CELTIC HERITAGE SAINTS

MARIAN KEANEY

VERITAS

First published 1998 by
Veritas Publications
7-8 Lower Abbey Street
Dublin 1

Copyright © Marian Keaney 1998

ISBN 1 85390 329 9

British Library Cataloguing
in Publication Data.
A catalogue record for
this book is available
from the British Library.

The poem by John Irvine on p. 66 was published by The Dolmen Press. Rights are now administered by Colin Smythe.

Illustrations: Jeannette Dunne
Design: Bill Bolger
Printed in the Republic of Ireland by Betaprint Ltd, Dublin

FOR
UNA, VINCE, URSULA, VIVIENNE

CONTENTS

acknowledgements

I wish to thank everyone who shared the Celtic heritage experience with me.

Ruth Illingworth gave me generous assistance with the background to Celtic Scotland and Cumbria. Staff at various libraries and visitor centres also assisted me in my information pilgrimage. They include: Clonmacnoise Heritage Centre, Co. Offaly; Lismore Heritage Centre, Co. Waterford; Ardagh Heritage Centre, Co. Longford; Westmeath County Library and Midlands-East Tourism HQ, Mullingar, Co. Westmeath; Arus Chilian Visitor Centre, Mullagh, Co. Cavan; St Colmcille Heritage Centre, Gartan, Co. Donegal; Bangor Heritage Centre, Co. Down; Glendalough Visitor Centre, Co. Wicklow.

For further help and assistance, my thanks to Tony Cox and Gearóid O'Brien, of Westmeath County Library, and the staff at Midlands-East Tourism HQ.

Special thanks to the Director and staff of Veritas Publications, especially Maura Hyland and Fiona Biggs, and to Jeanette Dunne for her delightful illustrations.

Marian Keaney

INTRODUCTION

Only a fool would fail
To praise God in his might
When the tiny mindless birds
Praise him in their flight

Early Irish Poem

Before St Patrick came to Ireland there was a Christian Celtic region in western Europe. It included Ireland, western Scotland, Wales, Cornwall, Brittany and southern Gaul. These areas were renowned for their hero worship, their mysticism, their art and their learning.

There was a learned class of druids, poets and lawyers in pre-Christian Ireland. When they converted to Christianity, many of these became monks and clerics, and they travelled down the European trade routes, preaching the Gospel message.

Irish monks brought learning, books and Christian ideals to Gaul and northern Italy. St Columbanus travelled widely in Europe and St Brendan and his sailor monks reached North America long before Christopher Columbus.

While women had many rights under Celtic or Brehon law, Christianity gave them an option other than marriage – they could become nuns instead and carry out distinct religious functions. St Brigid and St Hilda of Whitby are the most famous of these.

Celtic monks had very strong views on the preservation of the moral law, and frequently risked the anger of the powerful medieval rulers. St Columbanus was expelled from Burgundy when he reprimanded the king for his immoral behaviour. Queen Guilana of Würzburg hired killers to behead St Kilian.

Celtic Heritage Saints is a celebration of a great age of learning. World-famous illuminated books were produced in many monasteries – the best-known of these are the Books of Kells and Lindisfarne. The idea of the monk in his scriptorium illuminating his sacred manuscripts has a great fascination for me.

In recent years cultural tourism in Europe has centred around new heritage and visitor centres. In Ireland many new centres celebrate the golden days of Irish monasticism: Clonmacnoise, St Kilian Visitor Centre, Lismore Heritage Centre, St Colmcille Visitor Centre, Bangor Visitor Centre. New research on the Book of Kells has been undertaken at Trinity College Library, Dublin. School tours, heritage tours, tours for hikers and bikers are arranged to make the new heritage centres more accessible, so it is now easier than ever before to understand and appreciate the lives and work of the great Celtic saints.

Marian Keaney

St patrick, patron of ireland

The feastday of St Patrick, the patron saint of Ireland, is celebrated on 17 March.

Patrick was born in Wales, son of a church deacon called Calpurnius and the grandson of a Christian priest. His family are believed to have been Romans living in Britain. When he was sixteen years old, Patrick was captured during a raid by Irish pirates and was sold as a slave in Ireland. He is said to have herded pigs and sheep on the slopes of Slieve Mish in Co. Antrim for six years. He has described this experience in his autobiography, the *Confessio*. This is one of the few pieces of Celtic writing where the author can be identified. Patrick wrote:

> I had to stay all night in the forests and on the mountains looking after the sheep. I would wake to pray in all weathers, snow, frost, and rain. I felt no fear, nor did I feel sleepy.

During this time Patrick learned the Irish language and about the practices of the druids.

After six years of captivity, he had a dream in which God told him to leave Ireland and return to Wales. He escaped from his master, Milchu, and he was guided by angels for two hundred miles to a ship which took him to Britain.

Patrick was reunited with his family and then resumed his studies at Lérins in France. He studied with St Germanus, Bishop of Auxerre, until he was ordained priest, and continued to be guided by the saint for several years.

After his ordination, Patrick had several dreams in which God called him to return to Ireland as a missionary. His family did not approve of his plans to return to Ireland, but he was determined to do so, travelling through Britain until he reached Armagh about 432.

There had been Christians in Ireland before Patrick's return, but he remains the most important figure in the establishment of the Celtic Church there. His first church was a barn at Saul in Co. Down, given to him by a chieftain called Dichu.

When Patrick arrived at the Hill of Tara in Co. Meath, stronghold of the High King of Ireland, on the eve of Easter, he lit a great Paschal fire on the Hill of Slane, overlooking the Boyne Valley. It was the practice at that time of the year to put out all fires before the King's fire was lit at Tara.

The druids were very angry when they saw Patrick's fire at Slane. They told the King it would burn for ever. The King summoned Patrick to Tara. On the way there he and his followers chanted the hymn known as 'St Patrick's Breastplate':

> At Tara today in this fateful house
> I place all heaven with its power
> And the sun with its brightness
> And the snow with its whiteness
> And the fire with all the strength it has
> And the lightning with its rapid wrath
> And the winds with their swiftness along their path

King Laoghaire led his army out from Tara to challenge Patrick, but he escaped into the night with his disciples. Despite this bad start, Laoghaire eventually allowed Patrick to preach Christianity throughout his Kingdom and his two daughters became Christians.

Patrick travelled widely in Ireland, using the shamrock to teach the mystery of the Trinity. He established many new churches, but his main one was at Armagh. There is a legend in Sligo that the druids wanted to prevent Patrick from establishing a church at Shancoo, but the mists came down on the mountain and hid him so that the druids couldn't find him.

Once Patrick spent the forty days of Lent praying on Croagh Patrick in Co. Mayo. Demons came in the form of blackbirds to frighten him, so many of them that the sky grew dark. Patrick rang his bell to frighten them away, and they disappeared across the skies.

Patrick organised the Irish Church with powerful bishops, but he also encouraged the monastic life. Even before his death the Golden Age of Irish monasticism had begun.

Patrick died at Saul when he was about seventy. He is said to be buried at Downpatrick with St Brigid and St Colmcille. He had many followers, including St Benignus, who succeeded him, and St Fiach and St Mel, who helped him preach the doctrine of Christ throughout Ireland.

At the time of Patrick's death the Irish Church was firmly established and supported by bishops and priests. His Irish successors have played a prominent role in spreading Christianity far and wide. They founded the Church in Australia and New Zealand and strengthened it in England and the United States of America. Because of Patrick's zeal the Irish Celtic Church became a beacon of light in the Dark Ages in Europe. The Golden Age of the Irish saints had begun and its learning and civilisation influenced Europe for several centuries.

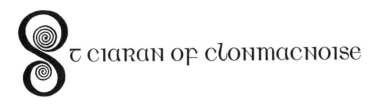St Ciaran of Clonmacnoise

St Ciaran's feastday is celebrated on 5 March.

In a quiet watered land
A land of roses
Stands St Ciaran's city fair.

These words from the poem 'The Dead at Clonmacnoise', by T. W. Rolleston, celebrate the famous monastery founded by St Ciaran. Clonmacnoise is situated on a beautiful elevated site overlooking a wide sweep of the River Shannon. It was such a famous centre of learning that it became known as the first Celtic university.

St Ciaran, the founder of Clonmacnoise, was born in 515. His father was a chariot-builder from Larne in Co. Antrim. His mother's name was Darera and she was a native of the south of Ireland. She met Ciaran's father on a visit to friends in south Westmeath. The couple settled there, later moving to Co. Roscommon.

Ciaran received the best education available at the time. His first teacher was a deacon called Justus. Later he studied at St Finian's famous school at Clonard in Co. Meath. Afterwards he led the life of a pilgrim for a time, visiting St Ninnad at Lough Erne, St Enda in the Aran Islands, and St Senan of Inis Scattery in the Shannon estuary.

Ciaran founded a number of monasteries on the islands in Lough Ree, and in 549 he came to Clonmacnoise where he founded his great monastery. It is built in a delightful area of river, bog and meadows, and can be reached by boat. In the early years monks travelled along the eiscirs or gravel ridges which formed major highways in Ireland at that time.

Clonmacnoise, like other monasteries such as Clonard and Durrow, had a large number of students. The monastic cultivation of art and learning reached a peak there. Scribes recorded Latin poems, and the Irish language, arithmetic, music, astronomy, astrology, mechanics and medicine were taught.

The monastic site at Clonmacnoise is said to have occupied an area of approximately ten acres. If you go to the Visitor Centre there you will soon understand how the monastery was organised. Extracts from the Annals of Ireland give an insight into the history of Ireland at the time. An excellent film gives details of the monks' everyday work, showing how they transcribed the scriptures or wrote history in the scriptorium.

Guided tours of the monastic site are available in several European languages. Over 100,000 visitors and tourists come to the monastery each

year. The visitors see the round towers – O'Rourke's Tower and MacCarthy's Tower – overlooking the Shannon. The Cross of the Scriptures, one of the world's greatest examples of stone carving, stands in the Visitor Centre, while replicas of this and other high crosses stand on their original sites.

Clonmacnoise is famous for its carved tombstones, hundreds of which are still preserved in the Visitor Centre. Many Irish kings had burial rights in Clonmacnoise; great processions of horse-drawn chariots would make their way with the royal remains to the monastic burial ground.

Sadly, Ciaran did not live to see his monastery's days of glory. He is said to have died of a fever seven years after his foundation of Clonmacnoise and was buried in Teampall Chiaráin, St Ciaran's Church. Its restored remains are in excellent condition today. Seven churches have survived at Clonmacnoise; one of these is the Nuns' Church, so it is clear that there were both monks and nuns at this monastery.

Some great books were written at Clonmacnoise, including *The Annals of Clonmacnoise* and *The Book of the Dun Cow*.

There was also a great school of metalwork at the monastery, one of the finest surviving pieces of which is the Clonmacnoise Crozier, now preserved in the National Museum of Ireland.

Students from England and the Continent of Europe came to study at Clonmacnoise, travelling along the rivers and the eiscirs to reach the monastery. 'Boatloads of young Englishmen go to Ireland to study grammar, geometry and physical sciences', wrote Abbot Aldhelm of Malmsbury in 685.

The glorious days of Clonmacnoise lasted for several centuries, but it fell into a decline after numerous raids by Irish and Viking invaders. However, in the nineteenth century the historian George Petrie outlined the importance of the monastic buildings there and the site was preserved by the Church of Ireland until it was handed over to the Office of Public Works.

Restoration of the monastic buildings continues and important archaeological discoveries have been made there. In 1996 a bridge which crossed the Shannon was found close to the ruined Norman castle nearby.

Pope John Paul II visited Clonmacnoise in 1979. So St Ciaran's 'city fair' remains important and active today, one of the great survivors of the Irish Celtic Church.

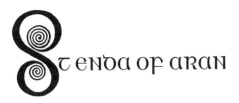# St Enda of Aran

St Enda's feastday is celebrated on 21 March.

St Enda belonged to one of the Irish royal families. He was son of Conall Dearg, King of Oriel. Tragedy struck him as a young man when the noble lady he hoped to marry died.

He decided to become a monk and travelled to Rome where he was ordained. When he returned to Ireland he built several churches in his father's Kingdom of Oriel.

Enda then visited his sister and her husband, the King of Cashel. The King presented the Aran Islands to Enda. These islands, off the Galway coast, are famous for their rugged beauty. About 483 Enda travelled to Aran from Co. Clare. He founded a monastery at Killeney on Inis Mór, the largest of the islands.

This monastery was so successful that saints and scholars later flocked to Aran. St Finian of Clonard, St Kevin of Glendalough and St Ciaran of Clonmacnoise are said to have visited Aran before founding their own monasteries. St Colmcille also visited Aran. St Brendan the Navigator came to St Enda for a blessing before he set off on his great voyage across the Atlantic Ocean.

The Aran Islands became famous as a place of worship. Soon they were widely known as 'Aran of the Saints'.

Enda founded several monasteries in the Aran Islands before his death in 549. Although his monastic rule is believed to have been very severe it had a major influence on the Irish Church at the time, and his successors, the Abbots of Aran, continued to rule his foundations until the year 1400.

Because of its island location Aran was not attacked by raiders as often as many monasteries on the mainland during Enda's lifetime. However, his monasteries were burned and robbed several times during the centuries after his death.

St Enda's name is remembered in the twentieth century. The ferry

Naomh Éanna was a familiar sight on its regular journeys from Galway to the Aran Islands. St Enda's well and altar are still preserved among the monuments on the islands and are visited by many people, both locals and tourists. There is also an altar at Cill Éanna. A number of inscribed stones date from the early monastic period on the islands.

Remains of a round tower, churches and high crosses can also be dated to the early monasteries on the Aran Islands.

In these many ways St Enda's monastic work is remembered today by tourists and pilgrims on the Aran Islands.

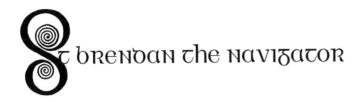

St brendan the Navigator

St Brendan's feastday is celebrated on 16 May.

Brendan was born at Fenit in Co. Kerry in 484, a descendant of a King of Ireland. He attended a famous school for boys founded by St Ita and he remained her friend throughout his life. Later he studied at the school of Bishop Erc and was ordained there.

St Brendan is the most adventurous Irish saint, well known for his legendary voyages. It is generally believed that he discovered America centuries before Christopher Columbus arrived there. Brendan always knew he wanted to sail the seas and he visited the Aran Islands to talk to St Enda about his plans. Afterwards he went to a mountain in Kerry to pray. Then he began to build his boat and prepare for a long voyage. The hull of the boat was covered in three layers of hide. When it was finished Brendan packed food for his journey – dried fish, grain and root crops.

He set to sea with a group of sailor monks. They landed at St Kilda in the Scottish Hebrides. The monks were half-mad with thirst when they found a safe landing place. There they restocked their food supplies. Today fishermen in the Hebrides pray to Brendan when they are in danger at sea.

Then St Brendan visited the Faroe Islands, off the north coast of Scotland. He landed at a bay in the Island of Storms.

He was at sea for a long time after leaving the Faroes. Then the sailor monks decided they would like to rest for Easter. They moored their boat and lit a fire on an island.

Suddenly the island shuddered as if there had been an earthquake, and it began to sink into the sea. The frightened monks raced back to their boat. They were just in time. When their 'island' disappeared under the sea, they realised that they had landed on a whale's back. The whale clearly had not enjoyed the experience either!

They set sail again, and reached the Shetland Islands where they met a solitary monk called Aibin who took them to his monastery and gave them food.

The sailors sailed away from the Shetlands, into dreadful weather. There were gales and hail on the way to Iceland where the volcano Hecla had erupted. As they went ashore, they were greeted by a stream of molten lava. Brendan and his monks were terrified and hurried away. After this adventure they returned to Ireland.

After a rest in Ireland Brendan and his monks sailed off again. This time they visited the Bahamas. They saw a calm blue sea, and many beautiful birds and fishes. They were convinced they had found the Land of Promise. Here they moored again, at a place now thought to be near Miami in Florida. The monks renewed their stores of fruit. They also collected gold and precious stones which they took with them to adorn sacred vessels in Ireland.

This was Brendan's last voyage. In Ireland his fame grew and many churches were dedicated to him. Brendan also built churches – the most famous was at Clonfert in Co. Galway. St Brendan's Cathedral in Clonfert is noted for its Romanesque doorway.

Several churches in Scotland are also dedicated to Brendan. It is said that he visited St Colmcille in Iona when he was eighty years old.

When he was more than ninety years old Brendan returned to his monastery in Clonfert. He died and was buried there in 577.

St Brendan wrote a book called *Navigatio Brendan* (The Voyage of Brendan). It is a tale of the wonders of the sea. The modern explorer Tim Severin sailed the route of Brendan's voyages in a primitive boat. The story of this adventure is called *The Brendan Voyage*.

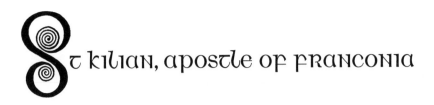

St kilian, apostle of franconia

St Kilian's feastday is celebrated on 8 July.

St Kilian was born at Mullagh, Co. Cavan, in 640. We know little of his youth, but his short life was filled with drama, and he became one of the most important Celtic saints in Europe.

Like many other Irish monks in the seventh century, Kilian decided to preach the Gospel in Europe. So he set out, dressed in a coarse grey tunic, carrying a staff and the Book of the Gospels.

First he travelled to Tuosist near Kenmare in Co. Kerry, and in 686 he sailed to Europe with his companions. They travelled along the Rhine and the Maine into Franconia, now part of Germany. There Kilian planted a cross on a hill overlooking the modern city of Würzburg.

Kilian told the people about Christianity, and soon became known as the Apostle of Franconia. He met the ruler of the Kingdom, Duke Gosbert, and became friendly with him. Gosbert invited Kilian to his castle near Würzburg. The Duke was married to his brother's wife Guilana, and when Gosbert became a Christian Kilian scolded him about this. When Guilana found out, she was furious.

She planned to destroy Kilian. She hired killers to do this. 'Cut off his head!' she commanded. So the killers drew their swords and beheaded Kilian and his companions. After the execution, the bodies were buried in a stable.

However, the death of Kilian haunted Guilana. At that time he was an important man, a powerful prince-bishop, so the people would not easily forget what had happened to him. The cult of the martyred saint grew and spread in Franconia and Kilian became the patron saint of Würzburg.

Meanwhile, Kilian's enemies fared badly. The man who had cut Kilian's head off went mad and tore out his teeth. Guilana was tormented by evil spirits that clawed at her throat until she died. Duke Gosbert was murdered by members of his family. His descendants were driven out of Franconia, and never ruled there again.

Kilian's fame continued to grow. Around 752 his body was found buried in the stable together with the bodies of his companions. Their remains were removed to a round church on the Marienburg. Soon pilgrims from all over Europe began to flock to the shrine of Kilian and his companions. By 1139 so many Irish pilgrims were coming each year that a special church was founded to cater for them. This church is called the Schotten-kloster of St James.

Throughout the centuries the people of Würzburg continued to celebrate Kilian's story and his memory. His name was remembered in many place names and schools. He was honoured in works of art in wood, metal and stone.

Kilian's relics and those of his companions were placed in a splendid casket which is still carried in procession through Würzburg on 8 July, Kilian's feastday. Many other honours were conferred on him. He was made patron of the wine-makers of Franconia in the nineteenth century. In the 1990s the Arus Chilian Heritage Centre in Mullagh was built with the help of Irish and European money. The Centre has a splendid collection of art relating to Kilian. It also shows an excellent short film on his life.

After St Kilian was murdered, his executioner cried out, 'Kilian, the holy man of God, is burning me with a terrible fire!'

This fire was so strong that it has continued to burn, keeping Kilian's name alive.

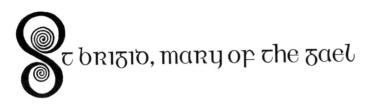

St bRIȝIð, mARy oꝬ the ȝael

St Brigid's feastday is celebrated on 1 February.

St Brigid is one of the three patron saints of Ireland. She is believed to be a native either of Faughart in Co. Louth or, perhaps, of Co. Kildare. Her father, Dubhrach, was a chieftain, and her mother's name was Brocessa.

As a child Brigid gave bread, butter, eggs and chickens to people in need. She loved the company of the wild animals and birds. Soon her friendship with animals and birds became known. She taught a wild fox to play games and tricks and she went to the court of the King of Leinster and gave the fox to the King. The King was amused by the antics of the fox.

Then her father decided it was time she got married. Dubhrach wanted Brigid to marry a poet. Poets were greatly honoured at the courts of the Irish High Kings. However, Brigid refused her father's request.

'I want to be a nun,' she said, 'I want to build a convent and a church, and I also want to build a school.' Dubhrach was very angry but Brigid told him she did not want a poet or anybody else as a husband. Instead she went with a group of her friends to become a nun.

Saint Mel, a friend of St Patrick, gave Brigid the nun's veil at Ardagh, Ireland's National Heritage Village, in Co. Longford. Today there is a well-known training centre and convent farm at Ardagh called St Brigid's Training Centre. A variety of farming and household skills are taught there.

Brigid then founded her principal monastery in Kildare. Hundreds of priests, holy women and scholars flocked there. There were monks as well as nuns in St Brigid's monastery.

Some nuns worked on the farm, others looked after the sick, while others copied sacred books.

Brigid did not have enough land for all the work that was going on in her monastery. She decided to ask the King of Leinster to give her some more land. She set off to meet him while he was out hunting at the Curragh of Kildare. The King got down off his horse to meet Brigid and her friends.

Brigid explained that she needed some more land. She would like good fertile land on which to feed her cattle. However, the King liked his forests and his hunting grounds. He did not want to give any land away.

Finally, Brigid asked the King, 'My Lord, will you give me as much land as my cloak will cover?' The King was amused and thought Brigid was making a joke. So, for fun, he agreed.

Then Brigid removed her cloak and spread it smoothly on the ground. The cloak began to grow and grow. The King was astonished, but the cloak continued to grow until it covered many acres of fertile land.

We cannot be sure how many acres the King gave to Brigid. In any case, we can be sure that he had plenty of land left for himself.

However, St Brigid had enough land to work at her monastery in Kildare. She continued to work there until she died in 525.

Later a cathedral, a round tower and a high cross were built in memory of the monastery founded by St Brigid.

St Brigid's feastday is held on 1 February, the pagan festival of spring. On that day people still make St Brigid's Crosses from woven rushes in her honour. There are many holy wells and places of pilgrimage dedicated to her throughout Ireland.

The Training Centre and the convent farm at Ardagh would have pleased St Brigid. The farm is an organic one. Cheese-making and bee-keeping are taught at the Centre. There is a St Brigid's Cross design in the wrought iron surround of the courtyard. Exchanges are arranged between Irish and European students to study rural life. In this way Brigid's influence remains important in Ireland and Europe.

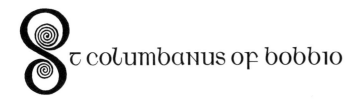 St columbanus of bobbio

St Columbanus' feastday is celebrated on 23 November.

St Columbanus was born in Leinster in the sixth century. He attended school at Killeigh in Co. Offaly and later went to the monastic school of St Comgall at Bangor in Co. Down.

He was ordained a priest in 572. After further sacred studies, he travelled to Europe with twelve companions from Bangor, among them St Gall and St Deicholus. They arrived in France about 590.

First they went to Burgundy, now famous for its fine wines. But at that time it was wild countryside, so the monks had to survive on roots and berries.

Columbanus founded three monasteries in Burgundy: Annegray, Luxeuil and Fontaines. These monasteries were famous for their learning, beautiful handwriting and illuminated copies of the gospels. Luxeuil was famous for several centuries and its rule became known throughout France.

Columbanus continued this work until Theodric, King of Burgundy, quarrelled with him. The two men fell out when Columbanus reproved Theodric for his immoral behaviour. Theodric expelled him from his kingdom.

Columbanus was given refuge by the King of Soissons who welcomed him to his kingdom. He founded more monasteries in Soissons. The best known was Rebais, which became a resting place for Irish pilgrims going to Rome.

After some time Columbanus travelled along the Rhine into Switzerland, where he stayed near Lake Constance. His companion St Gall became ill, and decided to rest. He built a cell near Lake Constance and became so famous in the area that he later became the apostle of the Swiss nation. The town and canton of St-Gall are called after him.

Meanwhile Columbanus crossed the Alps into Italy. He met King Agiluf of Lombardy, who gave him a wild stretch of land. It was on this site that Columbanus built his great monastery of Bobbio.

Bobbio became one of the most famous monasteries in Europe. Columbanus died there on 21 November 615 and his remains still rest in the modern church. The beautiful town of San Columbano was named in his memory.

One of Columbanus' friend, a monk called Jonas, wrote a Life of Columbanus which tells us many interesting things about the saint. According to the legends, squirrels and doves played in the folds of his cowl. Birds nestled in his hands, and the wild beasts obeyed his orders.

There is a painting of St Columbanus in a chapel at Fontaines. He is holding a scroll that reads:

'He sought a place, and built another monastery, which he named Fontaines.'

St colmcille, Dove of the church

St Colmcille's feastday is celebrated on 9 June.

Colmcille, scribe, poet and scholar, was born at Gartan in Donegal in 563. He was a prince of the royal Uí Néill family and could have been High King of Ireland if he had not decided to become a monk.

Colmcille studied the scriptures under St Finian of Moville. He learned the art of poetry from the bard known as Master Gemman, and he later became known as the Saint of Poets, patron and protector of the bards in Ireland.

Colmcille then went to Clonard in Co. Meath to study under another Finian. Finian of Clonard had studied widely in Ireland and Wales and was known as 'Teacher of the Saints of Eire'.

Colmcille was ordained priest by St Mobhi at Glasnevin in Dublin. When he returned to Donegal, his cousin, the High King of Ireland, gave him an island on the River Foyle. The learned men of the North, poets and musicians came there to meet Colmcille.

Great oak trees grew on the island and Colmcille later founded his first monastery at Derry, which means 'the place of the oaks'. He wrote a poem in praise of Derry:

> Dearly I love Derry for
> its gentle fields and brightness
> and the fair angelic host
> filling it with lightness.

Colmcille founded many monasteries in Ireland, including Durrow in Offaly, Swords in Dublin, Colmcille in Longford and Kells in Meath. He sang in praise of his foundations:

Beloved are Durrow and Derry,
Beloved is Raphoe the pure,
Beloved are Swords and Kells.

Colmcille's great love of learning often got him into serious trouble. He secretly copied a rare and precious book belonging to Finian of Moville. When Finian heard about this he was very angry and demanded the copy. Colmcille refused, but Diarmuid, the High King, made a famous decision against him:

To every cow its calf, to every book its copy.

He ordered Colmcille to give his copy to Finian. Colmcille was not pleased with the King's decision and he fought a great battle at Cúl Dréimhne in Sligo known as 'the Battle of the Books'. He was later filled with remorse for this misdeed.

In 563 Colmcille left Ireland to go to Scotland. He landed on the island of Iona where he built the monastery which later became famous as the chief seminary of Britain and the burial place of monks, scholars and many Kings of Scotland.

The monastery at Iona had a chapel, a kitchen, a dormitory, a hospital and, of course, a scriptorium where the sacred books were copied and illuminated. Baoithín was Colmcille's chief scribe and he ornamented his writings.

The monks also worked on the monastery farm. 'There are three labours in the day', said Colmcille, 'prayers, work and reading.' The Iona monks were also great sailors, and they explored the bays and gulfs around the rugged Scottish coast. When the Vikings raided Scotland, they found books, crosses and bells which were made by the Iona monks.

Colmcille left Iona for a while to work among the Picts at Inverness. In the meantime the work of Iona spread until there were several new foundations on the island and in mainland Scotland.

Colmcille visited Ireland once more to settle a dispute among the Irish bards. He spent the rest of his life on Iona and the surrounding islands. One day, when he was going from the monastery to the barn, he sat down to rest. A white horse from the monastery farm came up to him. The horse knew that Colmcille was going to die soon and placed his head in the saint's lap and cried until great tears flowed down onto Colmcille's cloak. Then Colmcille went to the scriptorium to write. When he came to Psalm 34 he wrote, 'Here at this page I must stop'. The next morning his monks found him lying in front of the altar where he had died.

Years later the monks brought Colmcille's body back to Ireland and buried it in Downpatrick beside St Patrick and St Brigid.

The 1400th anniversary of Colmcille's death was celebrated in 1997, with celebrations at Iona, at his birthplace in Gartan in Donegal, at Durrow and at Kells. The celebrations surrounding the anniversary sparked off an enormous interest in the wider Celtic Church, and Colmcille's place in it is assured.

His spirit is especially vibrant in the Irish-speaking region of Co. Donegal. St Colmcille's Church of Ireland is situated at Glencolmcille, near a hiding-place said to have been used by the monks during Viking raids.

Colourful tales about Colmcille still abound in this area of spectacular cliffs and seascapes. Some demons are said to have sought refuge in the glen when St Patrick was preaching Christianity there. They remained firmly in control until the arrival of St Colmcille a century later. Then there was consternation among the demons. One of them threw a holly stick, killing one of the saint's companions. The stick hit the ground and immediately grew into a holly bush. The demons fled at this remarkable sight. Not to be outdone, Colmcille gave chase, throwing stones and even his own bell after the demons. They fled across the cliffs and into the sea.

When Colmcille had driven out the demons, he introduced Christianity into the area.

Inscribed standing stones known as Turas Cholmcille, or Colmcille's

Pilgrimage, are among the striking features of Glencolmcille. There is a poem by Colmcille in the Bodleian Library at Oxford:

> Let not the old glen be violated,
> The site of the stone slabs of heaven.

This is a powerful appeal for the preservation of Glencolmcille and its standing stones.

New books about Colmcille and about the famous illuminated manuscripts associated with him were published to celebrate the anniversary year. Many more stories about Colmcille can be found in these publications.

St Finian of Clonard

St Finian's feastday is celebrated on 12 September.

According to tradition, Finian was born on the slopes of Mount Leinster in Co. Carlow, and it is said that the birds of Ireland gathered in joy at his birth. He is regarded as the father of Irish monasticism and is known as 'Master of the Saints of Ireland'.

As a young man Finian founded three churches in Ireland before going to Wales to study the monastic life. He studied under St Cadoc at Lancarfan in Glamorganshire. He was impressed by another of Cadoc's pupils, St Gildas, who was critical of the wealth of the British bishops. Finian later went to Tours for further studies.

By this time Christianity had spread throughout the Celtic regions of Ireland, Scotland, Wales, Cornwall and South Gaul. This Celtic area was united by trade and literacy. Finian's vision was of a Church that would deliver books and ideas together with the cargoes of wine and salt along the Atlantic seaboard. Irish monks would travel these routes, bringing learning, books and Christian ideals to central Europe. Learning had always been important in Ireland, where there had been a learned class of poets, lawyers and druids in pre-Christian times.

Finian founded his first monastery at Aghadoe in Co. Wicklow. He felt that the monastic life was well suited to Ireland, and because the country was made up of so many small kingdoms he could be sure of royal patronage.

He went to visit St Brigid in Kildare, and was probably very surprised when she presented him with a gold ring. At first he refused it, but when Brigid insisted and told him that the ring would be of use in the future, he graciously accepted this unusual gift. Shortly afterwards Finian met his friend, Caisin, who told him that he needed an ounce of gold to pay a ransom to the King. Brigid's ring weighed about that, and while Finian didn't wish to give it away so soon, he knew Caisin needed help. When Caisin presented the ring to the King, he was given his freedom.

Eventually Finian went to Clonard in Co. Meath, on the River Boyne, and decided to settle there. He founded his most important monastery there and it became the most significant monastic school of the sixth century. It is said that at one time more than three thousand monks studied there.

At Clonard the monks learned the art of writing old Irish in Latin script. As a result of the influence of Clonard, many manuscripts containing Gaelic poetry, law, texts, grammar, stories, saints' lives and histories were prepared in other monasteries.

Many monastic founders came to Clonard to learn from Finian. His influence spread across Ireland, through Britain and Celtic Europe.

As the monastic school of Clonard continued to grow, more students came and built their huts around the main monastery. Finian soon became known as 'Tutor to the Saints of Ireland'.

Under Finian's influence the Irish Church began to be governed along monastic lines, rather than under the rule of a bishop. This was a huge departure from the type of structure established by St Patrick. Finian himself was an abbot as well as a bishop, and he lived the same life of work and study as the rest of the monks.

It is widely believed that twelve famous bishops, who founded some of the best-known monasteries in Ireland, were educated at Clonard.

They include:

St Ciaran of Offaly
St Ciaran of Clonmacnoise
St Colmcille of Iona
St Brendan the Navigator
St Brendan of Birr
St Colum of Terryglass
St Molaise of Devenish
St Cainnech of Aghaboe
St Ruadhan of Lorrha
St Mobhi of Glasnevin
St Suinell of Cleenish
St Ninnad of Inishmacsaint

Several stories are told about these saints while they were studying at Clonard. St Ruadhan had a miraculous lime tree. Sweet-tasting fluid dropped from its branches, which was so special that whoever drank it could taste whatever they wanted to. The other monks entertained their guests with this drink, and Ruadhan was probably very popular.

One day, the poet Master Gemman complained to Finian that his crops were poor because his land was not fertile. 'I do not ask for gold, silver or precious clothes', he said to Finian, 'but soon I hope that my land will improve.' Finian told him to scatter some very special water over his fields. St Gemman did this and rich crops soon grew again. Gemman is remembered today as a poet and farmer and as the tutor of St Colmcille of Iona.

Finian died of plague about 549, so he didn't live to see the results of his monastic teaching. His students continued to found other monasteries throughout Ireland, so Clonard had a major influence on the other monastic schools.

Clonard lasted a long time, surviving even the Viking invasions and the violent quarrels of the Irish chieftains. It also flourished throughout the Norman invasions, when great de Lacy strongholds such as Trim and Delvin were built all over the Kingdom of Meath. However, the great monas-tery was destroyed during the suppression of the monasteries in the sixteenth century, and scarcely any trace of the famous monastic school survives today. However, its outline can be seen from the air and, more importantly, its influence is reflected in other famous centres of learning such as Clonmacnoise and Iona.

St Finian is remembered today in the Catholic church at Clonard, where events from his life are depicted in the magnificent stained-glass windows. There are life-sized wooden statues of St Finian and St Etchen carved in Italy. Facing on to the main Dublin–Sligo road there is a dramatic marble statue of St Finian, carved by the Italian sculptor Carlo Nicole. It depicts St Finian holding the torch which has become a symbol of his ministry.

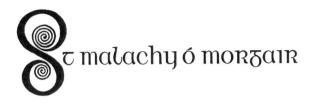# St malachy ó morgair

St Malachy's feastday is celebrated on 3 November.

Malachy was born in 1094, probably in the city of Armagh. Both his parents came from noble and learned families. His father is said to have been 'chief lector of Armagh and of the west of Europe', and his mother's family owned the lands of the great monastic school at Bangor. Malachy's older brother, Giollacríost, became Bishop of Clogher. His father died when Malachy was about eight years old.

Malachy studied under the best teachers, and was ordained around 1119. Some years later he was ordained Vicar in the Archdiocese of Armagh. His task was to bring about changes in the Irish Church which had suffered greatly during the centuries of Viking invasions. While doing this work, Malachy went to Lismore to study Church law. There he was taught by Malchus, the learned Bishop of Lismore.

When Malachy returned from Lismore, he established a monastic community in Bangor and was appointed Abbot there. His foundation was near the site of the famous monastery founded in Bangor by St Comgall a few centuries earlier.

In 1124, when he was only thirty years old, Malachy was appointed Bishop of Connor. At that time the famous schools and monasteries in the diocese had been burned down. Many of the libraries were destroyed during the Viking invasions and Malachy's task was to improve this situation.

When the city of Connor was destroyed by an Irish King, Malachy had to flee from his diocese. He went to Munster with 120 of his monks. There King Cormac of Desmond gave him a site for another monastery.

When it was safe for him to do so, Malachy returned to Bangor. He was made Archbishop of Armagh and Primate of all Ireland.

Malachy continued to found monasteries. His next foundation was at Downpatrick. Then he decided to go to Rome to meet the Pope. He travelled to Scotland, then to York, then on to France, where he stopped at the

Cistercian monastery of Clairvaux. Its founder, St Bernard, had a great interest in mysticism and had wide influence in Europe. He was also interested in sacred music, art and gothic architecture.

Malachy and Bernard soon became good friends. Then Malachy travelled to Rome where he met Pope Innocent II. By that time he wanted to join Bernard's monastery at Clairvaux. However, Pope Innocent refused him

permission, and told Malachy to return to Ireland to organise the bishops and clergy.

Malachy visited Clairvaux on his journey home and left five of his monks with St Bernard. Bernard agreed that they could join the Cistercian order and could then return to Ireland.

In 1142 a group of French and Irish Cistercian monks arrived in Ireland. They founded the great abbey of Mellifont in Co. Louth, which became famous for its magnificent buildings and its learned monks. The Cistercian monks were skilled in farming and in building methods.

Mellifont was the largest abbey in Ireland at that time. The consecration ceremony was attended by many kings and nobles, including the High King of Ireland.

Other Cistercian abbeys, such as Newry, Co. Down, Bective, Co. Meath and Boyle, Co. Roscommon, were founded in the following years.

Then Malachy decided to go to Rome again. He travelled through Scotland and founded a Cistercian monastery there. King David of Scotland arranged to meet him because he was impressed with his work.

Malachy travelled on to Clairvaux. There St Bernard was again delighted to meet him. 'On his arrival a joyous light shone on us', Bernard wrote afterwards. However, after a short time Malachy caught a fever. He died some days later in the company of St Bernard, who was greatly distressed by the death of his friend.

Later Bernard wrote a biography of the great churchman. When Bernard died five years later, his remains were laid beside those of Malachy. Their heads are still preserved in the high altar of the Cathedral at Troyes.

Malachy was canonised in 1190 by Pope Clement III.

After his death, the number of Cistercian abbeys in Ireland continued to grow. By 1200 there were twenty-six, the largest at Jerpoint in Kilkenny, where there were 1,300 monks.

Many Cistercian monasteries were destroyed during the reign of King Henry VIII. However, the ruins of some of these abbeys have been preserved as national monuments by the Office of Public Works in Ireland. Thousands of tourists and visitors come to the restored abbeys of Mellifont and Boyle every year. In other monasteries the traditional Cistercian work continues – at New Mellifont, at Roscrea and at Mount Melleray.

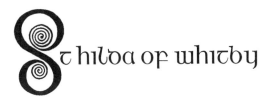

St Hilda of Whitby

St Hilda's feastday is celebrated on 17 November.

St Hilda is revered as a great leader and reformer in the Celtic Church, and her importance has been recognised by the famous scholar and historian, Bede the Venerable.

Hilda was born in Northumbria in 614, a princess of the Deiron dynasty, grand-niece of King Edwin of Northumbria. She spent her early childhood in East Anglia, then moved back to Northumbria, with its beautiful lakes.

Hilda was baptised by the Welsh monk, St Paulinus, when she was thirteen years old. Paulinus came to Northumbria in 629 and King Edwin and Queen Ethelbruga converted to Christianity soon afterwards. Edwin was later defeated in battle by pagan kings, who attempted to destroy Christianity in Northumbria.

In 633 Edwin's nephew, Oswald, decided to take on the pagan kings. The armies met at Hexham, near Hadrian's Wall. It is said that Oswald had a vision of St Colmcille before the battle. He won the battle and established his seat at Bamburgh. He had been educated at Iona and he sent to Iona for a great missionary to bring Christianity back to Northumbria.

Some time afterwards, St Aidan left Iona with twelve companions and established his monastery at Holy Island, which later became better known as Lindisfarne. The monastery, situated across the sea from Oswald's court at Bamburgh, soon became famous as a place of beauty, work and prayer.

While her royal relatives worked for the advancement of Christianity in the Kingdom of Northumbria, Hilda privately continued her Christian life. First she travelled to her cousin King Anna's realm of East Anglia. The Gallic Church, an offshoot of the Irish Church, was influential in this area. While in East Anglia, Hilda decided to join the monastery of Chelles in France, where her sister Hereswitha was a member of the community.

However, when St Aidan met Hilda he recognised her abilities as a leader and persuaded her to return to Northumbria. When she agreed, he placed her in charge of a small nunnery on the River Wear.

She later became abbess of a monastery of monks and nuns at Hartlepool where she developed a rule or way of living to bring more order into the lives of the community. After spending some time in Hartlepool Hilda was transferred to Whitby in Yorkshire, another monastery of monks and nuns who lived apart, but sang the Divine Office together in church.

Whitby became famous under Hilda's rule. 'Even kings and princes asked for and accepted her advice', Bede wrote. She encouraged her students to study Scripture, and several of her monks became bishops, one of whom was St John of Beverley.

Hilda also encouraged the creative arts. She became patron to the poet Caedmon, who had been a servant at the monastery but who became a monk at her suggestion.

Because of its reputation for learning, Whitby was chosen as the location of the Great Synod in 664, summoned by King Osby of Northumberland to settle a dispute over the date of Easter. Other matters discussed at the synod related to the consecration of bishops and the organisation of dioceses. Many important churchmen attended the synod, including Bishop Colman of Lindisfarne, Bishop Chad of Lichfield, Bishop Wilfrid of York and Bishop Agilbert of the West Saxons.

King Osby settled the disputes in favour of the Roman Church, although Hilda and her religious had sided with the Scots in favour of Celtic customs. It is said that she disapproved of the part played by Wilfrid at the synod, and she later had a role in removing him from the power he had gained in Northumbria.

Hilda survived the Synod of Whitby by about seven years, during which time she was very ill. St Bede tells us how a nun called Begu heard a bell ringing in her sleep one night and saw Hilda's soul going to heaven. She called the other nuns together and they prayed in the church until daylight, when the monks came with news of Hilda's death.

St Hilda's relics were kept at Whitby until the Viking invasions, when they were either destroyed or moved to some unknown place.

St Hilda's feastday is now celebrated on 17 November throughout Britain, where her important role in the Christian Church has been acknowledged by scholars and historians.

St Carthage of Lismore

St Carthage's feastday is celebrated on 15 May.

Very little is known about the early life of St Carthage. When he first arrived in Lismore in Co. Waterford, he was met by a holy woman who prophesied that he would found a 'lios mór' or 'big fort' there.

The prophecy was fulfilled in 633 when Carthage founded his monastery there. It soon became known for its learning and was visited by many Irish saints. Within a few decades it was renowned throughout Britain and Europe, becoming as famous as Bangor and Clonmacnoise. King Alfred of Wessex studied there in the ninth century, and St Malachy, then Primate of Armagh, visited the monastery before travelling to Clairvaux.

The main section of Lismore monastery was situated in a dramatic position on a high crag. The students lived in little huts made of mud and wattles, stretching for nine miles along the banks of the Blackwater. At the height of its fame there were twenty churches in the monastery.

As in other famous Celtic monasteries there was a scriptorium, and there was also a school of metalwork, where artefacts like the famous Lismore Crozier were made. The Crozier and the Book of Lismore were found hidden in the walls of Lismore Castle in the nineteenth century.

Today there is little trace of St Carthage's famous monastery. Lismore Castle, part of which dates from the early seventeenth century, was built on the site of the monastery and medieval towers and monastic ruins were incorporated into the general construction.

The monastery of Lismore is remembered today in the Lismore Heritage Centre, a fine building in classical style where visitors are treated to an award-winning multi-media presentation, which takes them on a fascinating journey through time, beginning with the arrival of St Carthage in 636 and finishing in the present day.

All major works on Irish monasticism published today stress the important role of Lismore in the Irish Church and as a major place of learning. St Mochuda is also associated with Lismore and St Declan founded the famous monastery of Ardmore, another lovely location on the river Blackwater in Co. Waterford.

St Margaret of Scotland

St Margaret's feastday is celebrated on 16 November.

Margaret was an English princess brought up in the court of King Stephen of Hungary, who was related to her mother. When Margaret was about twelve years old she came to England to the Court of King Edward the

Confessor. After the Norman invasion of England Margaret took refuge in Scotland with her mother. They were welcomed by King Malcolm Canmore, the 'Great Leader'.

This was around 1070. Margaret was in her early twenties, beautiful and accomplished. King Malcolm proposed marriage and the royal wedding took place at Dunfermline Castle in Fife when Margaret was twenty-four.

The royal couple were very happy together. Margaret assisted the King by carrying out works of justice, mercy and charity. She often visited the sick and took care of them herself. During Advent and Lent the King and Queen would entertain hundreds of poor people, serving them with dishes from their own table. Malcolm was always ready to take Margaret's advice and he placed her in charge of his household. He also consulted her on matters of state, and her influence was soon felt throughout Scotland.

Queen Margaret promoted the arts and encouraged education and the study of religion. With the King's help she founded several churches, the most important of which was Holy Trinity at Dunfermline. She helped reorganise the Scottish Church after the upheaval caused by the Viking invasions. She held synods where new laws regarding Sunday and Easter observance were made.

The Queen formed an embroidery guild among the court ladies. Soon her quarters became 'a workshop of sacred art', producing vestments and church furnishings.

Margaret and Malcolm had six sons and two daughters. Three of her sons, Edgar, Alexander and David, became Kings of Scotland, and David was revered as a saint. Their daughter Matilda married King Henry I of England, and it is through this marriage that the present British Royal Family traces its line from the early kings of Wessex and England. Matilda was popularly known as Good Queen Maud.

Margaret always made time for prayer and reading the scriptures. Her famous Book of the Gospels, with its fine jewelled casket, is now among the treasures of the Bodleian Library at Oxford. Although the book is supposed to have fallen into a river, it is largely undamaged.

In 1093 King William Rufus made a surprise attack on Alnwick Castle, one of the principal Scottish strongholds, and killed members of the garrison protecting the castle. King Malcolm and Prince Edward were slain.

At this time Queen Margaret was very ill in bed. When Prince Edgar return-ed from Alnwick, he assured her that his father and brother were well, but she suspected the worst. She was overcome with sadness and said to her servants, 'perhaps this day a great evil has befallen Scotland'. Four days later, on 16 November 1093, Margaret died, aged forty-seven. She was buried in the church of the Abbey of Dunfermline which she had founded with her husband.

Margaret was canonised in 1250 and was named patron of Scotland in 1673. After her canonisation her remains were moved to a new and splendid tomb in the Lady Aisle. Lights were kept burning before it until 1560. During the Reformation the lights were extinguished and the tomb was desecrated. Mary Queen of Scots rescued the saint's head, and when Mary had to flee to England it was entrusted to a Benedictine monk. He passed the precious relic on to Jesuit missionaries who brought it to Antwerp. In the seventeenth century it was taken to the Scottish College at Douai, eventually disappearing during the French Revolution. During these turbulent centuries portions of the remains of Margaret and Malcolm were brought to Spain, and in the nineteenth century Bishop Gillis brought a relic back to Scotland.

St Dympna of Gheel

St Dympna's feastday is celebrated on 15 May.

St Dympna is said to have lived in the seventh century, the daughter of a pagan Irish king and a Christian mother. She was baptised in secret.

As a young girl Dympna led the life of a fairytale princess, but when her beautiful mother became ill and died, tragedy entered the girl's life. Her bereaved father wanted another beautiful woman to replace the wife he had admired so much. After some time he decided to make Dympna, who greatly resembled her mother, his wife and queen. Although women had an important place in Celtic society, with well-defined legal rights, there was no precedent for a sensitive situation like this. Medieval kings and nobles assumed extraordinary rights and functions.

Dympna soon realised that she was in an impossible situation. She was determined not to give in to her father's demands for an incestuous relationship and she fled the court with her chaplain, Gerebern, and a courtier and his wife.

The party settled at Gheel in Flanders, near the present-day Belgian city of Antwerp. Dympna devoted herself to the care of the sick, hoping that she was safe from her father's strange obsession.

However, her father was trying to find a way of locating Dympna so that he could impose his will on her. Finally, through some clever detective work, he managed to trace her hiding-place. In the seventh and later centuries noble and royal families often had their own coinage and it was easy to follow the trail of Dympna's spending on her journey to Gheel.

The King crossed the sea in pursuit of his beautiful daughter and repeated his royal command that she marry him. Once again she refused and, outraged, he cut off her head. He also slaughtered her faithful travelling companions.

According to legend, many miracles took place after the dreadful murders. Local people, appalled by what had happened, discovered two

marble tombs which they believed had been brought by angels to honour Dympna.

These two coffins were preserved at Gheel and are said to have contained the bodies of Dympna and Gerebern. As the years passed the relics of the two came to be revered, and grave robbers tried to steal them, succeeding with those of Gerebern, which they brought as far as Sousbeck in the Rhineland, where they are now kept in a special shrine.

In and around Gheel Dympna's name and courage were remembered. Through several generations the people of Gheel provided out-patient facilities for the specialised care of the mentally ill. St Dympna is believed to have been responsible for many cures of insanity and epilepsy. Today there is a famous mental hospital at Gheel, and there are altars in her honour at Hasselt, St Quentin and Herck-la-Ville in Belgium.

Dympna's feastday is 15 May, and a pilgrimage to her shrine is held on that day each year. Her relics are now kept in a silver reliquary in the church named after her.

St Kevin of Glendalough

St Kevin's feastday is celebrated on 3 June.

Glendalough is one of the best-known Celtic pilgrimage sites. The main features of the famous monastic settlement are a round tower, churches, lakes and mountains. Glendalough means 'the valley of two lakes'.

The monastery was founded by St Kevin, who was born in the middle of the sixth century to the noble family of Dal Mesincorb. From an early age the boy was renowned for his special gifts. When he was twelve he was sent to Kilnamanagh Monastery in Co. Dublin where he studied under three holy men, Eogan, Lochan and Erna.

Kevin ran away from the monastery and hid in the Dublin mountains. Soon he came to Glendalough and climbed to the Upper Lake, where he settled in the hollow of a tree and lived on a diet of fresh herbs and water. He loved the solitude at Glendalough and he stayed there until his teachers found him and brought him back to Kilnamanagh, where he continued his studies and was eventually ordained a priest.

When Kevin founded his first monastery at Cluainduach he was joined by several companions. But Glendalough was his special place and he

returned there as soon as possible. He founded his monastery in the Lower Valley where two rivers meet. After a while he decided to become a hermit and he set out alone to the Upper Valley where he built a small cell between the mountain and the lake. He lived there for about four years, eating berries, plants and nuts and some fish from the sparkling waters of the lake. Wild animals came from the mountains and woods to keep him company. Soon they were so tame that they would come to drink water out of Kevin's hand.

> The speckled trout would swiftly glide
> To the reedy water side,
> And there the mountain deer would stand
> To eat the green moss from his hand.

> The snarling wolf and savage boar
> Lay down together at his door,
> And so defied all natural laws
> About the cave where Kevin was.

> JOHN IRVINE

There are many stories from the animal kingdom about Kevin and his friends. One day, when a hunter and his dogs were chasing a wild boar, the boar raced into Kevin's cell for safety. Imagine the hunter's surprise when he found Kevin saying his prayers with a number of birds perched on his head and shoulders! The hunter called off the hunt and the boar escaped.

Kevin had a few adventures with monsters in the lake. It is said that when he was praying at night in the cold water a very lively monster tried to distract him by lashing its tail around the lake – perhaps the monster was trying to tell Kevin that he should have some sense and go to bed to keep warm! On another occasion Kevin banished a monster from the Lower Lake to the Upper Lake.

Kevin worked many miracles at Glendalough and crowds of people came to visit him there. Some women are supposed to have tried to distract Kevin from his prayers. One, Kathleen, annoyed him so much that he threw her into the lake.

St Kevin died in 618 when Glendalough was just coming into its heyday as a monastic school with about a thousand pupils.

Like many other monasteries, Glendalough was plundered by the Vikings, but its fame has lived on. Its most famous abbot was St Laurence O'Toole who became Archbishop of Dublin in 1163.

After a disastrous fire in 1398 the monastery gradually declined until the nineteenth century. Restoration of the buildings was carried out and Glendalough has been well-maintained since then. The whole site now lies within Glendalough Forest Park and is open to visitors throughout the year.

St Comgall of Bangor, Light of the World

St Comgall's feastday is celebrated on 10 May.

Comgall was born of noble parents in Co. Antrim about 517. It is said that St Patrick had foretold his birth about sixty years earlier.

Comgall studied under St Finian at Clonenagh in Co. Laois, later going to Glasnevin where he met St Colmcille and St Ciaran of Clonmacnoise. He then returned to Northern Ireland and founded his monastery at Bangor in 555.

The early monastery was a cluster of wooden buildings looking out to the sea. It grew rapidly and soon there were seven choirs of monks who chanted the Lord's praises all day. At the height of its fame there were about four thousand monks at Bangor, which became known as 'the Vale of Saints'. Many years later it was described by St Bernard of Clairvaux as 'truly sacred, the nursery of saints'.

Comgall's rule is said to have been very strict. At first he ate only one meal each day, but he improved his diet when his health began to suffer.

Wonderful gardens have always been a particular feature of the great monasteries and convents, and Bangor, with its abundance of fruit, vegetables, herbs and flowers, was no exception. One day St Comgall found thieves stealing the fruit and vegetables from his monastery garden. Comgall had no sympathy for criminals and his response was quick and decisive – he prayed to the Lord to deprive them of their sight.

So, the next time the clever thieves crept into the monastery garden, they were immediately blinded. They stumbled around, but couldn't find the way out. Eventually they fell into the gooseberry bushes and they howled all night. Comgall left them there until they begged for mercy and promised they would never steal from the monastery garden again. Comgall finally let them have their sight back, and they fled.

On another occasion the monastery ran short of grain. A neighbouring farmer named Cruidhe had a fine stock but refused to sell it to the monks. Again, Comgall wasn't going to take any nonsense. He prayed for evil to fall on the farmer, and that night a big colony of mice appeared and ate thirty wagonloads of grain.

The monastery larders were bare again when St Colmcille came to visit Bangor. This time Comgall prayed for some food. A huge shoal of fish in Belfast Lough swam close to the monks who caught plenty of them and cooked them for a mouth-watering feast.

Comgall visited Dalriada in Scotland and the Kingdom of the Picts in the east of that country. He founded a monastery at Tiree near Iona, and stayed there for a while. His companion Molaing travelled across from Bangor and together they accompanied St Colmcille when he went to see the Pictish king, Brude. The meeting was successful and King Brude allowed the monks to spread Christianity throughout his kingdom.

Two of Comgall's monks founded a monastery at Paisley. About a century later Bangor monks founded the monastery of Applecross. During the next three centuries monks from Bangor played an important part in spreading Christianity in Scotland, although many of the foundations were destroyed during the Viking invasions.

Bangor didn't escape invasions either – nine hundred monks were slaughtered by sea pirates during a raid.

The famous monastery is now completely destroyed, although some important relics survive, including the Bell of Bangor, preserved in the Bangor Heritage Centre, and the Antiphonary of Bangor, which is housed in the Ambrosian Library in Milan.

sources

Chadwick, Nora, *The Celts*, London: Penguin, 1991.

Cremin, Aedeen, *The Celts in Europe*, Sydney: Sydney University Centre for Celtic Studies, 1992.

De Paor, Máire and Liam, *Early Christian Ireland*, London: Thames & Hudson, 1958.

Delap, Dara, and other partners of the Northumbria Community, *Celtic Saints*, ed. Ann Lockhart, Hampshire: Pitkin Pictorials, 1995.

Flanagan, Laurence, *A Treasury of Irish Saints*, Belfast: Blackstaff, 1995.

Gleann Cholm Cille, *Guide Book*, Glencolmcille (Donegal): Oideas Gael, 1997.

Harbison, Peter, *Irish High Crosses*, Drogheda: The Boyne Valley Honey Company, 1994.

Hickey, Elizabeth, *The Irish Life of St Finian of Clonard*, Meath: Meath Archaeological and Historical Society, 1996.

Ireland, Office of Public Works, Manning, Conleth, *Clonmacnois*, Dublin: Stationery Office, 1994.

Jones, Alison, *The Wordsworth Dictionary of Saints*, Hertfordshire: Wordsworth, 1994.

Keaney, Marian, *Irish Missionaries from the Golden Age to the 20th Century*, Dublin: Veritas, 1985.

Ó Floinn, Raghnall, *Irish Shrines and Reliquaries of the Middle Ages*, Dublin: Country House in Association with the National Museum of Ireland, 1994.

Ó Fiaich (Cardinal), Tomás, *Columbanus in his own words*, Dublin: Veritas, 1974.

Rodgers, Michael, and Losack, Marcus, *Glendalough: A Celtic Pilgrimage*, Dublin: Columba, 1996.

Scott, A. Brian, *Malachy*, Dublin: Veritas, 1976.

Stokes, Margaret, *Three Months in the Forests of France*, London: Bell, 1895.

Wallace, Martin, *A Little Book of Celtic Saints*, Belfast: Apple Tree Press, 1995.

More Stories About Celtic Saints...

St Brigid – The girl who loved to give

Patricia Egan

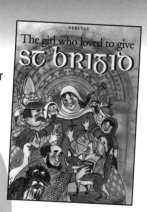

You might consider it a blessing to have a saint living in your house, but St Brigid was a source of trouble and annoyance to her father. She firmly believed the rich should give to the poor, and she duly gave away all that she and her father owned. St Brigid's story is delightfully brought to life by Patricia Egan and through the wonderful illustrations of Jeanette Dunne. *St Brigid – The girl who loved to give* is suitable for children aged between seven and ten years old.

ISBN 1 85390 222 5 • £1.50 • 24pp Paperback

Saint Patrick and the Snakes

Patricia Egan

The legendary life of Ireland's patron saint takes a whole new twist as Patricia Egan focuses on St Patrick's banishing of the snakes out of Ireland. She talks of how the snakes used to sneak up and steal food from people's kitchens, how they danced and laughed as the druids attempted to place a spell on them and how they created havoc and trouble wherever they went. *Saint Patrick and the Snakes* contains some very witty illustrations and is suitable for six- to nine-year-olds.

ISBN 1 85390 059 1 • £1.95 • 36pp Hardback

• *Available from Veritas and all good bookstores* •

VERITAS

7/8 Lower Abbey Street, Dublin 1
Tel (01) 878 8177 • Fax (01) 878 6507 • e-mail sales@veritas.ie

Also: Stillorgan (01) 288 9231 • Cork (021) 500 400 • Ennis (065) 28696
Sligo (071) 61800 • Letterkenny (074) 24814

UK: Veritas, Lower Avenue, Leamington Spa, Warwickshire CV31 3NP
Tel (01926) 451 730 • Fax (01926) 451 733

Stories About Monastic Life...

THE BOY AND THE BOOK

A Story of Early Christian Ireland

Francis McCrickard

The Boy and the Book is a vivid and exciting story of early Christian Ireland, rich in the details of life in the monastic settlements. This is the tale of Diarmuid from his youth as a shepherd, to his life in the monastery and his mission to rebuild his monastic life after the death and destruction brought about by Viking invaders. In addition to the story, there are instructions for a number of activities and exercises which will deepen the young reader's understanding of life as it was at that time.

ISBN: 1 85390 047 8 • **Price:** £1.00 • 104pp Paperback

The Call of the Wood Pigeon

A Day in the Life of a Monk in Pre-Viking Ireland

Richard Roche

A monk's life in pre-Viking Ireland was not all prayer and penance. There was work to be done to meet the day-to-day needs – in the kitchen, in the garden, in the fields and, most importantly, in the scriptorium. *The Call of the Wood Pigeon* is a superb book for children and ideal for anyone learning Irish because it is a parallel text. Overall, this is a tale that gives us a glimpse of monastic life in ancient Christian Ireland – the kind of life that gave Ireland the title of Island of Saints and Scholars.

ISBN: 1 85390 047 8 • **Price:** £1.00 • 24pp Paperback

Available from Veritas and all good bookstores

V ERITAS

7/8 Lower Abbey Street, Dublin 1.

Tel: (01) 878 8177 • **Fax: (01) 878 6507** • e-mail: sales@veritas.ie

Also: Stillorgan (01) 288 9231, Cork (021) 500 400, Ennis (065) 28696, Sligo (071) 61800 & Letterkenny (074) 24814.

UK: Veritas, Lower Avenue, Leamington Spa, Warwickshire CV31 3NP

Tel: (01926) 451 730 • Fax: (01926) 451 733

VERITAS BOOKS FOR CHILDREN

More Alive-O Stories and Poems

Clare Maloney
Jeanette Dunne (Illustrator)

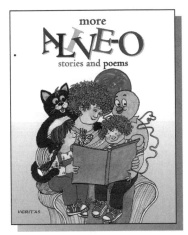

More Alive-O Stories and Poems is a unique book for children aged between 4 and 6 years.

The stories follow the adventures of Finchy and Fluffy, Globetrotter the goldfish, Jemima the scarecrow, and other characters familiar to this age group from their *Alive-O* schools' programme.

The story of Globetrotter's second day out at the beach, the story of Jemima the scarecrow whose best friend was a crow called Bertie, and the story of Finchy and Fluffy and their Neighbours, are all colourfully illustrated. Poems about summer, autumn, spring and the twelve days of Christmas cake, as well as poems about the cutlery family, the bear who couldn't sleep, the old man named McCua and his many pets, and the poem about how the tadpole develops into a frog are all told so that the full creative imagination of children is allowed to develop naturally.

Children love to dream and *More Alive-O Stories and Poems* will feed their imaginations.

1 85390 338 8 • £4.99 • 48pp Paperback

Available from Veritas and all good bookstores

VERITAS

7/8 Lower Abbey Street, Dublin 1
Tel (01) 878 8177 • Fax (01) 878 6507 • e-mail sales@veritas.ie

Also: Stillorgan (01) 288 9231 • Cork (021) 500 400, • Ennis (065) 28696 • Sligo (071) 61800 • Letterkenny (074) 24814
UK: Veritas, Lower Avenue, Leamington Spa, Warwickshire CV31 3NP
Tel (01926) 451 730 • Fax (01926) 451 733

welcome to www.veritas.ie

OUR SUBJECT CATEGORIES CHANGE REGULARLY AND FEATURE THE BEST BOOKS AVAILABLE IN EACH OF THOSE AREAS

FIND OUT more about these and any other **Veritas titles**

directly on our Website.

Order over the **Internet** from ANY of our listed categories.

You can also enquire about **ANY** book of interest to you.

Why not joint in on <u>our on-line</u> discussion group.
Our **CHAT GROUP** allows you to share and air your views with others.

Even if you have nothing to say,
the **chat group** makes fascinating reading!!!

Contact us NOW at our website...

http://www.veritas.ie

for further information contact email: marketing@veritas.ie or phone (01) 878 8177

This book aims to help beginners play flute simply and easily. The book includes 76 brightly colored pictures with fingering positions for the flute, with pitch names and staff notations. The musical notes included are:

C C#/Db D D#/Eb E F F#/Gb G G#/Ab A A#/Bb B of the 4th, 5th, and 6th octave.

Cut out the fingering charts and use them as a visua... students. The size of the cut-out is 6.5x10 inches (16... own piece of paper. You can post these cut-outs on th... One side of the cut-out shows the connection between t... and the reverse side depicts the same fingering scheme snown on a flute itself. Under the flute pictures, you will also find the fingering combinations depicted with the names of the flute keys. You simply choose the style that is more understandable and comfortable for you.

THE PARTS OF THE FLUTE

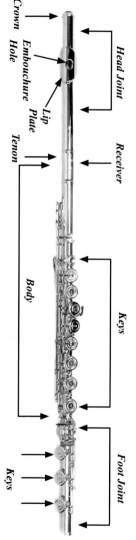

Crown
Embouchure Hole
Head Joint
Lip Plate
Tenon
Receiver
Body
Keys
Foot Joint
Keys

FLUTE FINGERING

TH - Left Thumb Finger
LH1 - Left Index Finger
LH2 - Left Middle Finger
LH3 - Left Ring Finger
LH4 - Left Pinky

RH1 - Right Index Finger
RH2 - Right Middle Finger
RH3 - Right Ring Finger
RH4 - Right Pinky

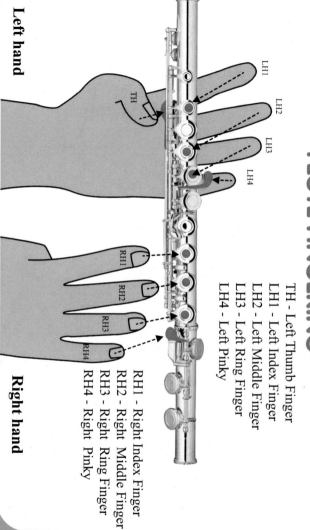

Left hand

Right hand

TH
LH1
LH2
LH3
LH4
RH1
RH2
RH3
RH4

D1507348

FLUTE FINGERING CHART

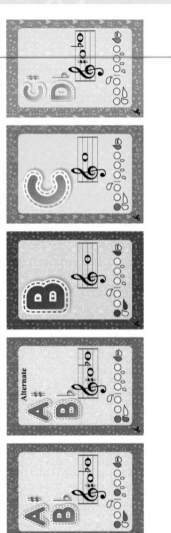
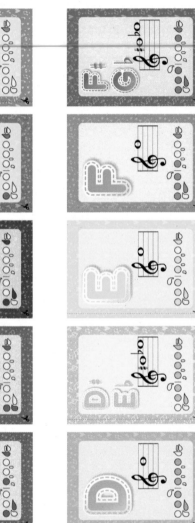
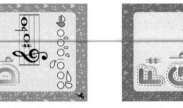

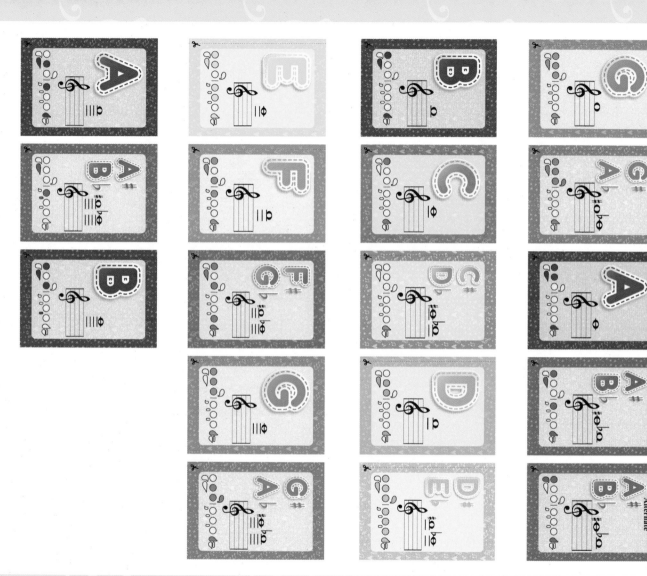

FLUTE KEY NAMES

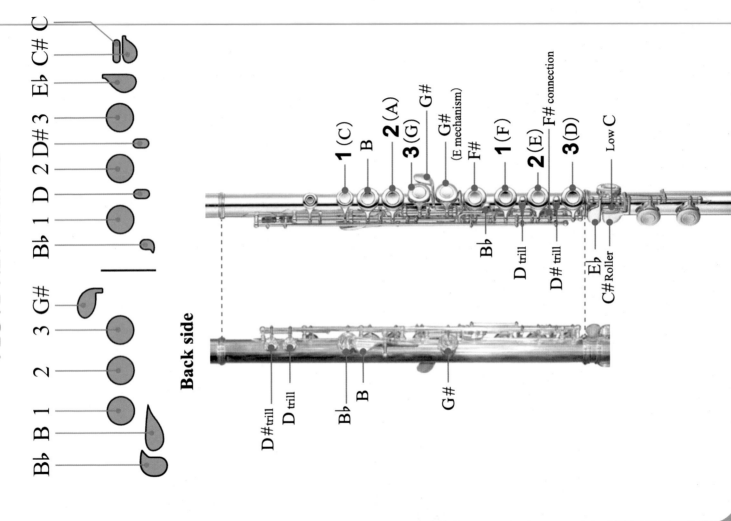

Back side

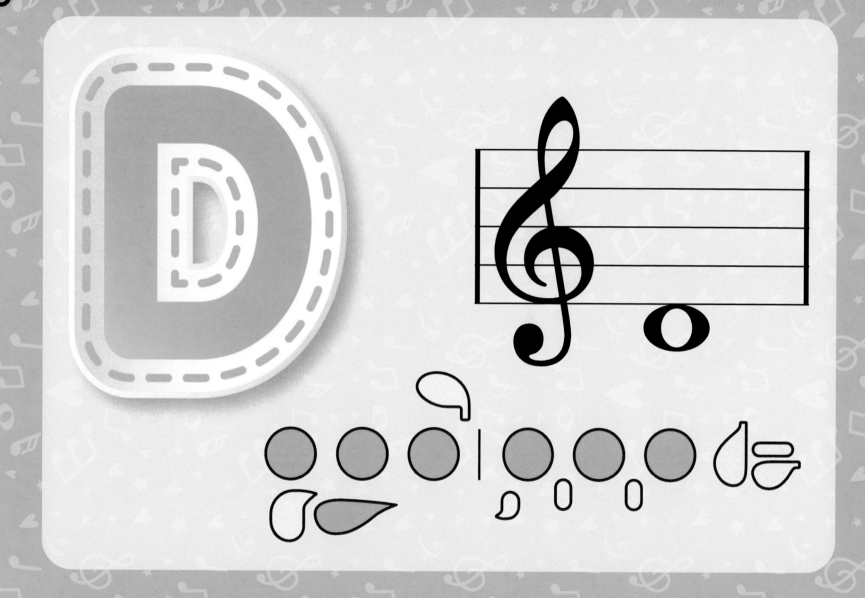

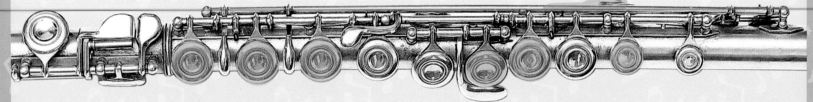

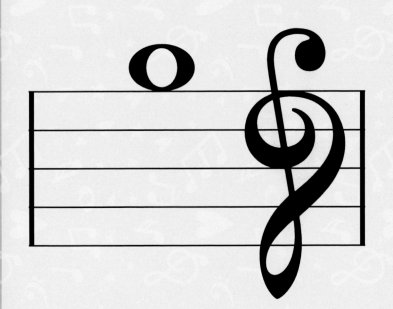

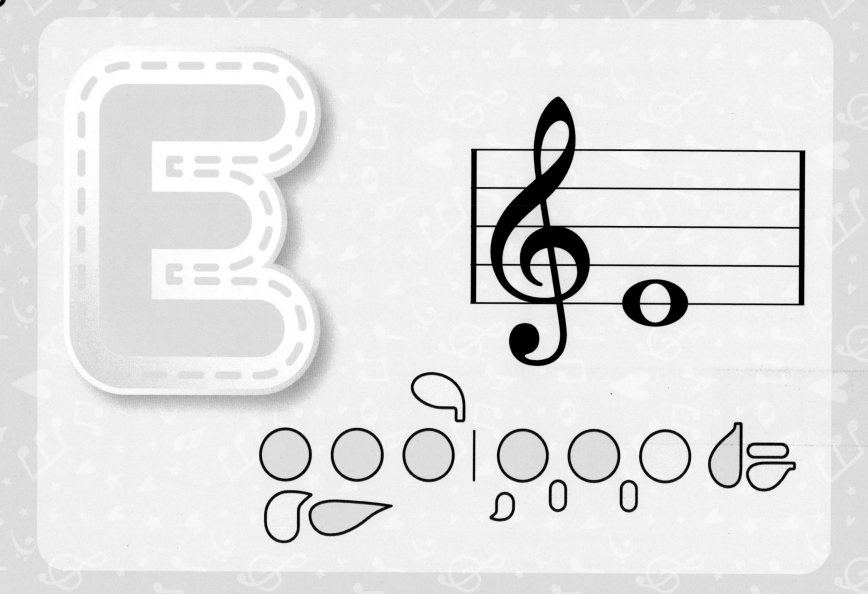

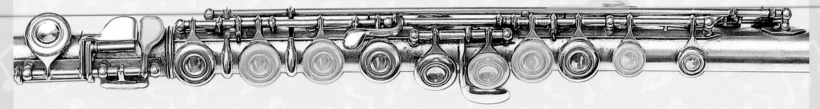

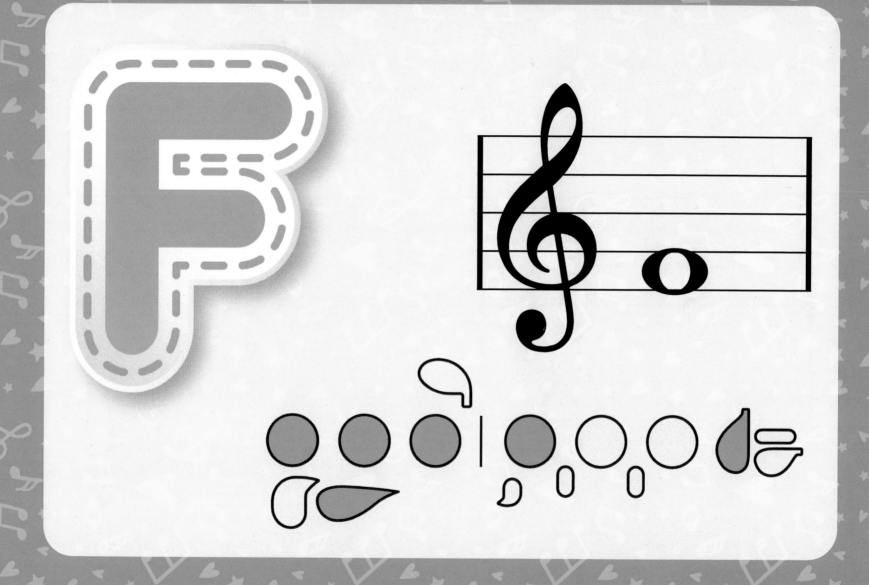

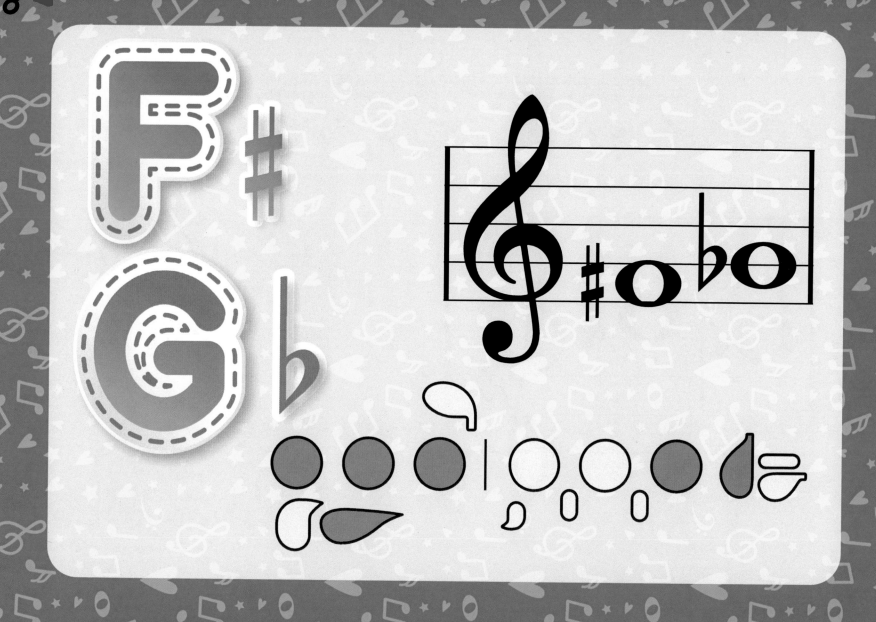

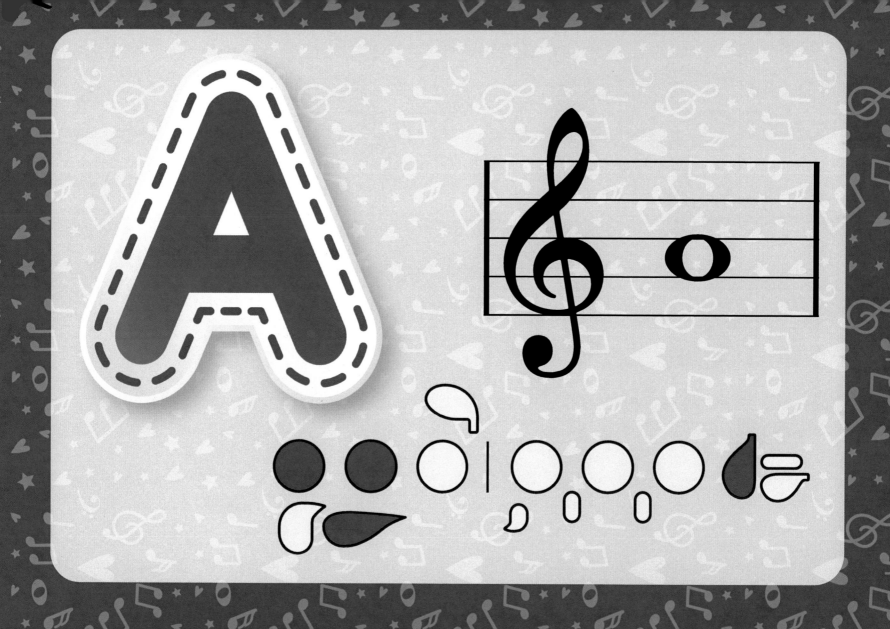

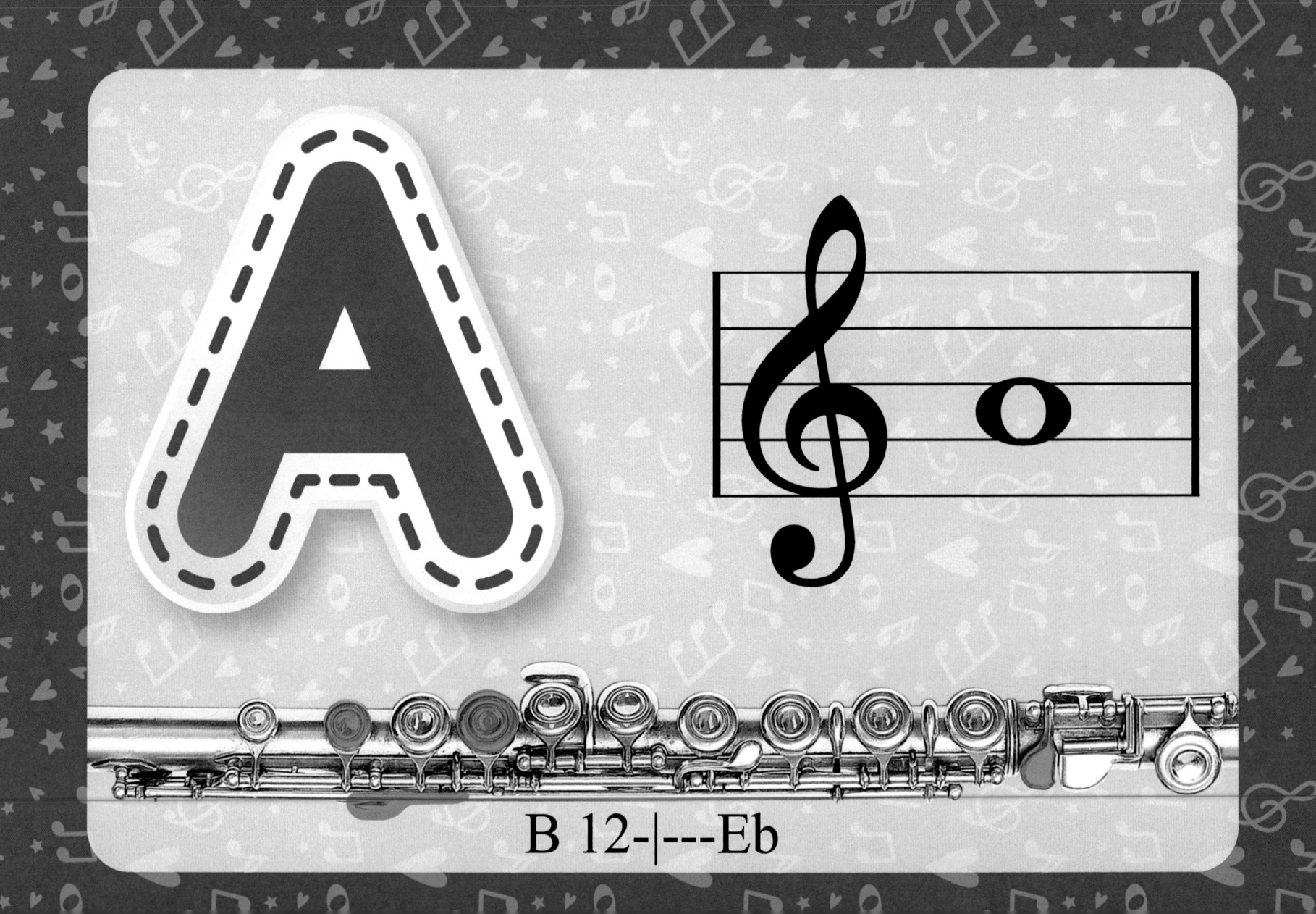

B 12-|---Eb

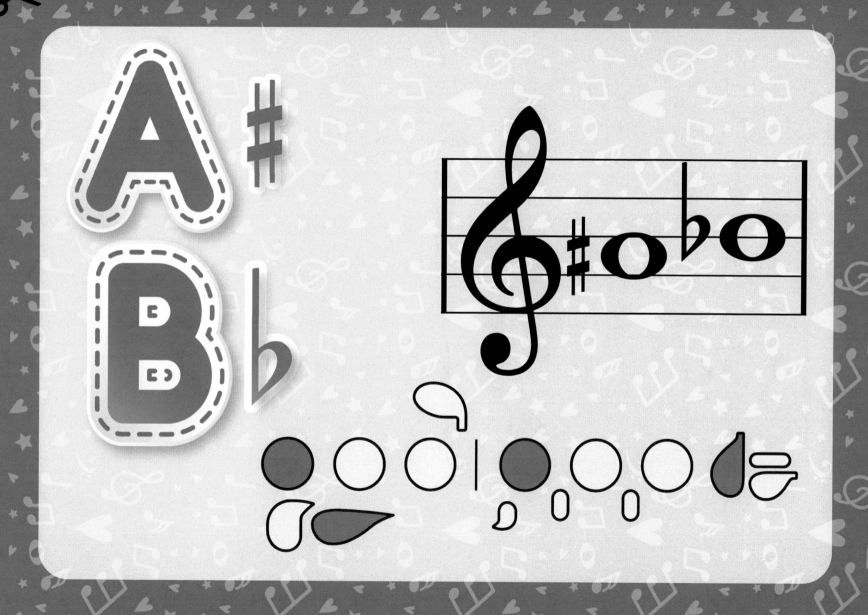

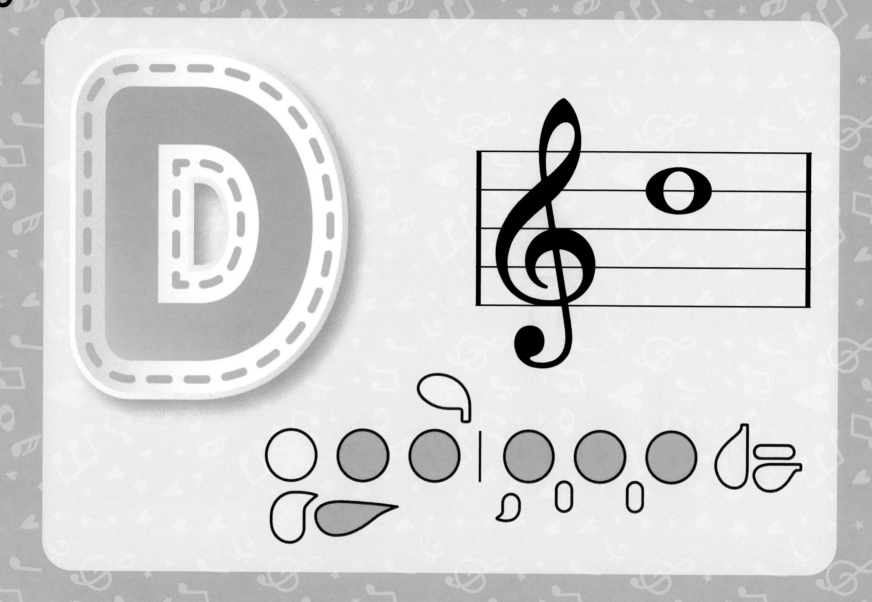

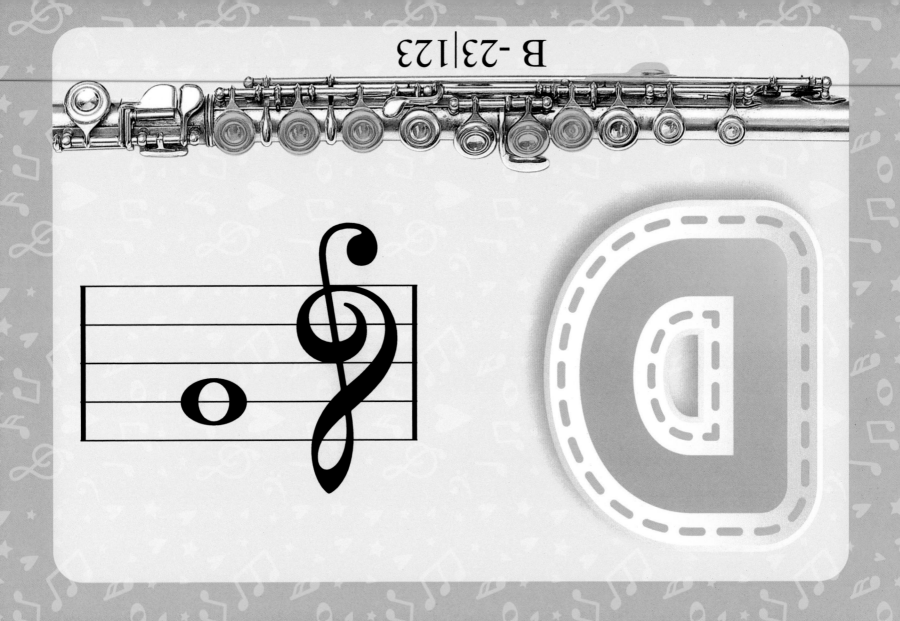

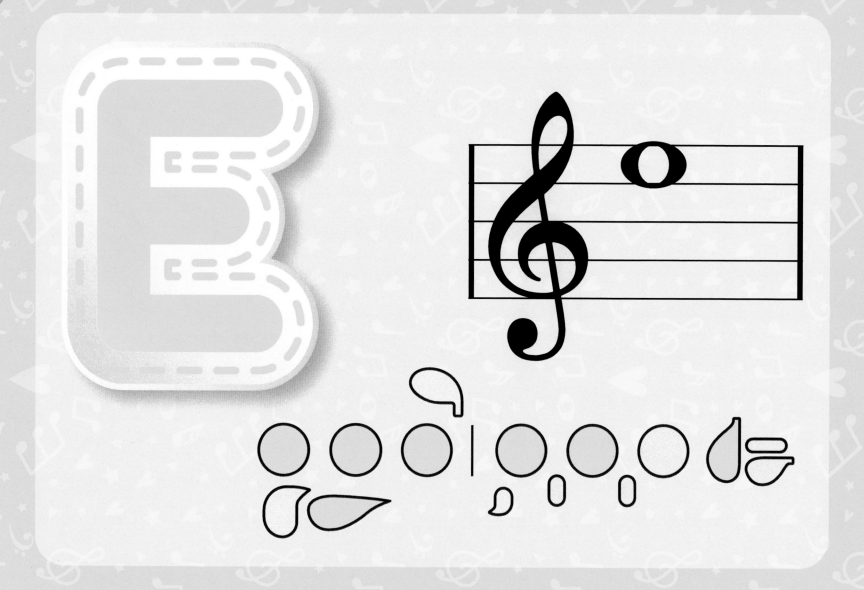

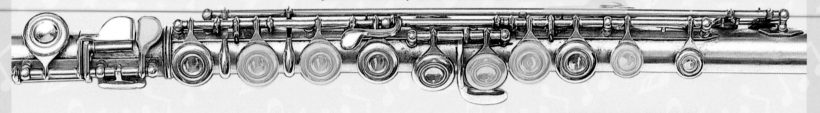

B 123|1--Eb

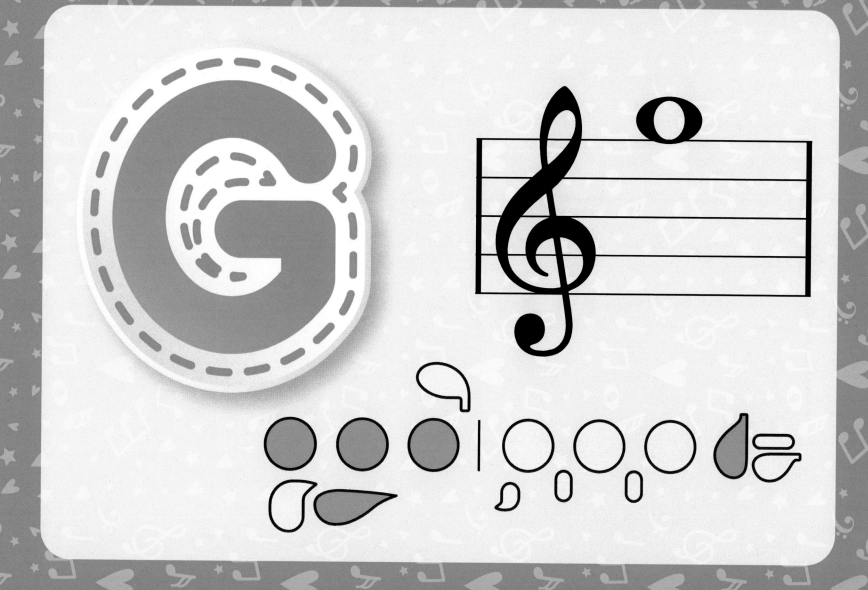

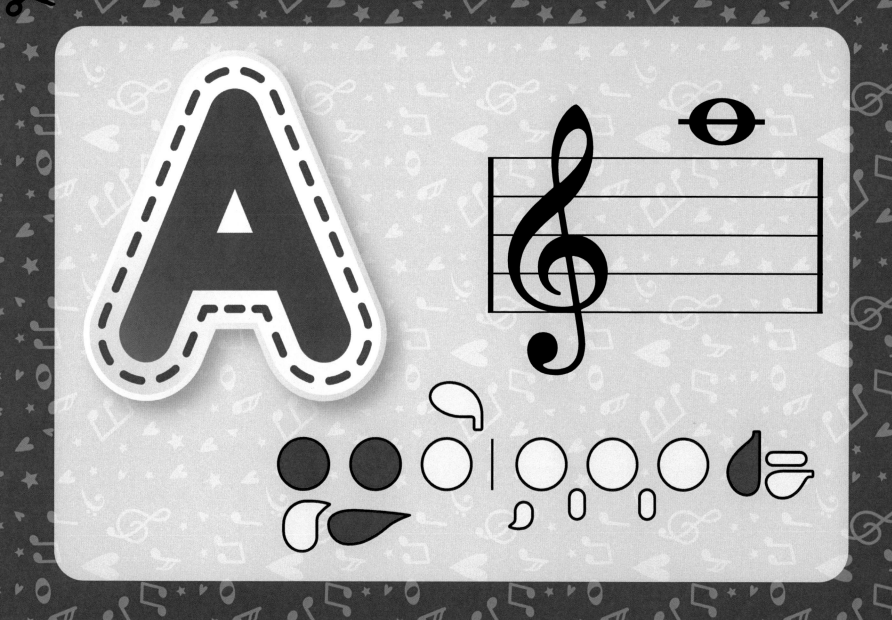

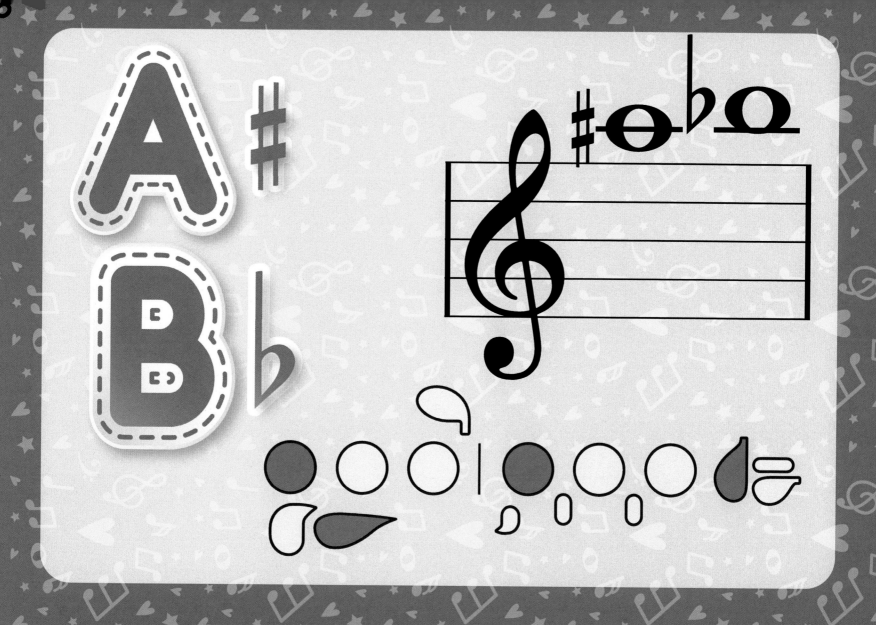

B 1--|1--Eb

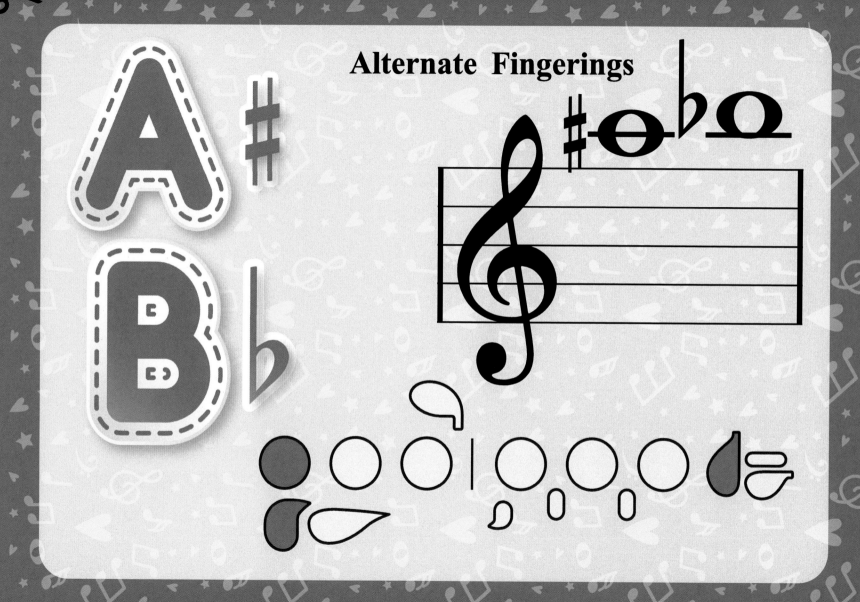

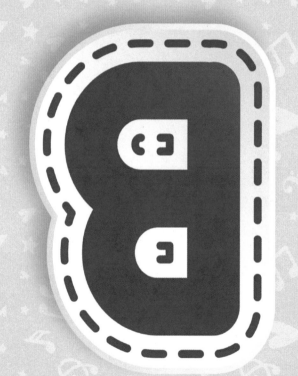

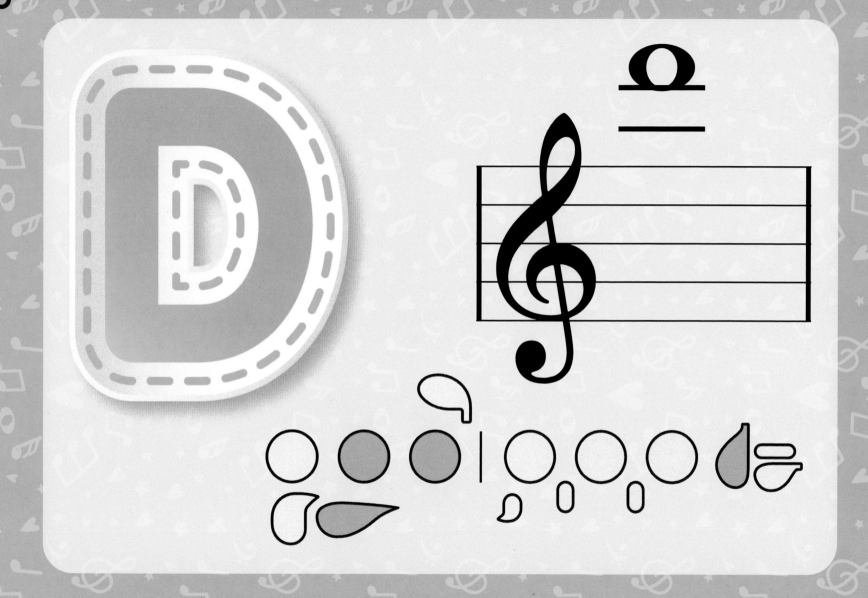

E

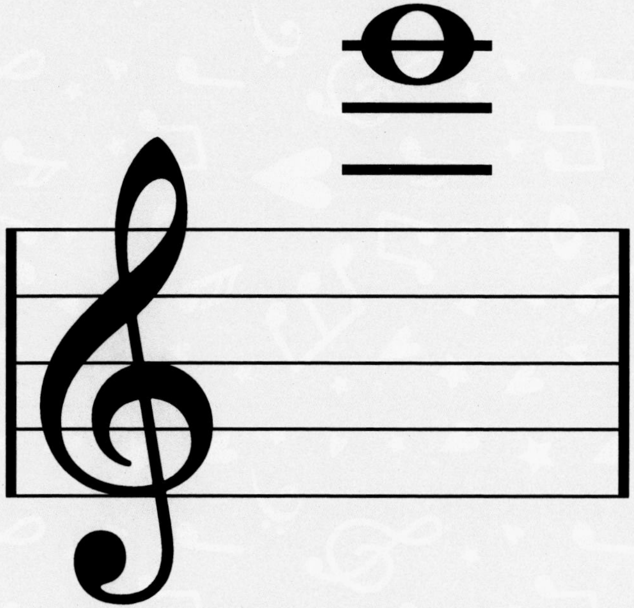

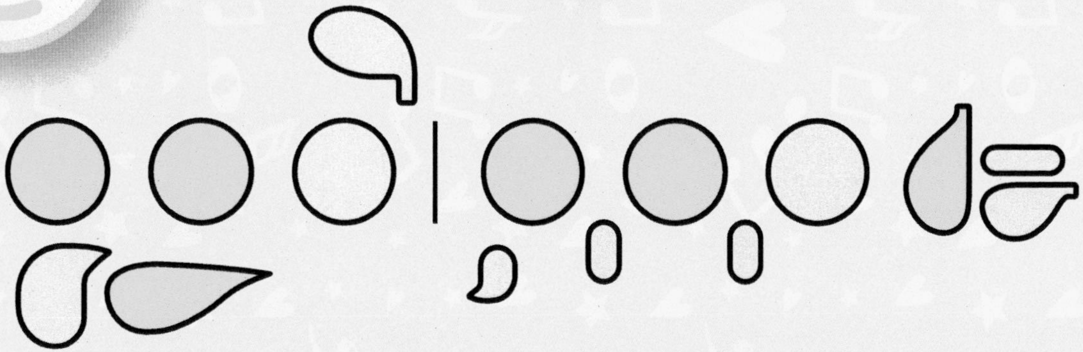

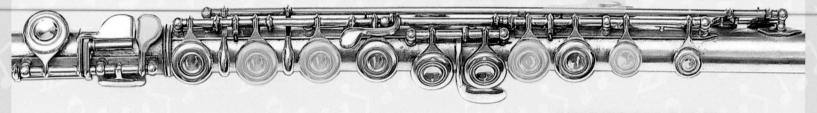

B 12-|12-E♭

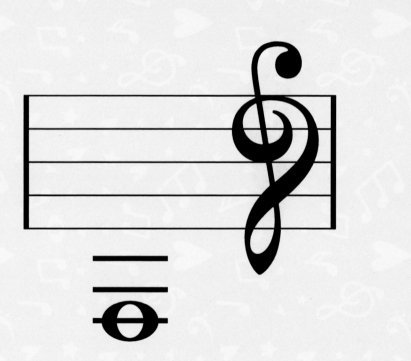

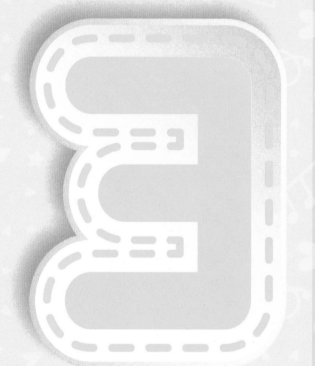

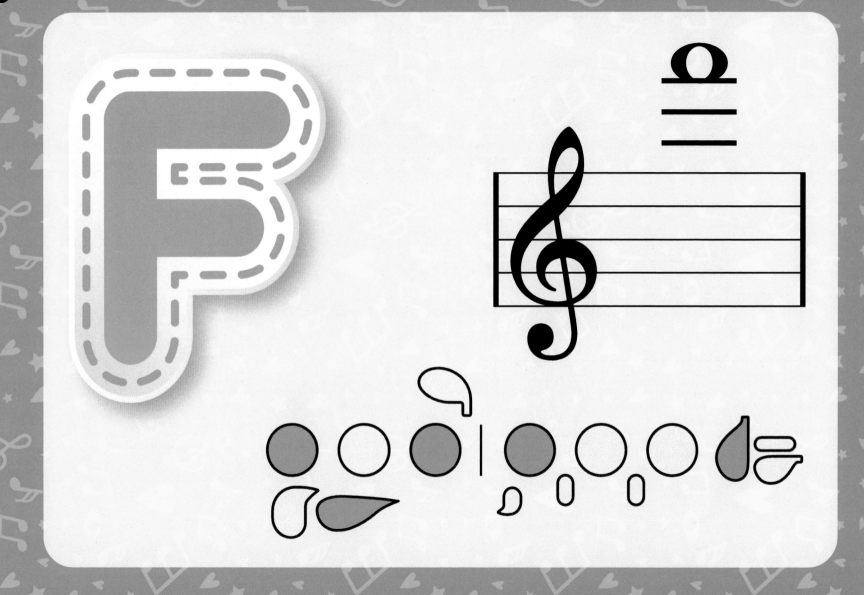

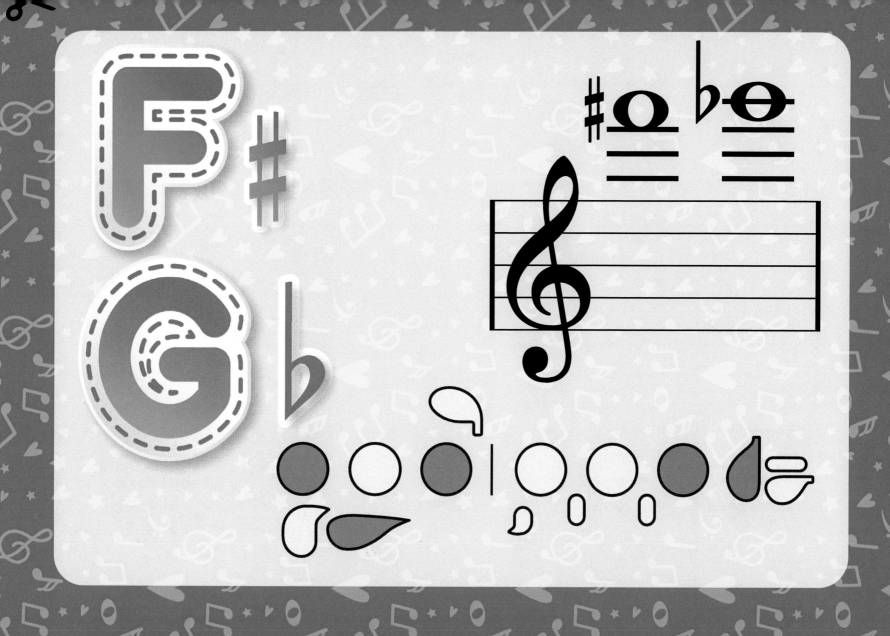

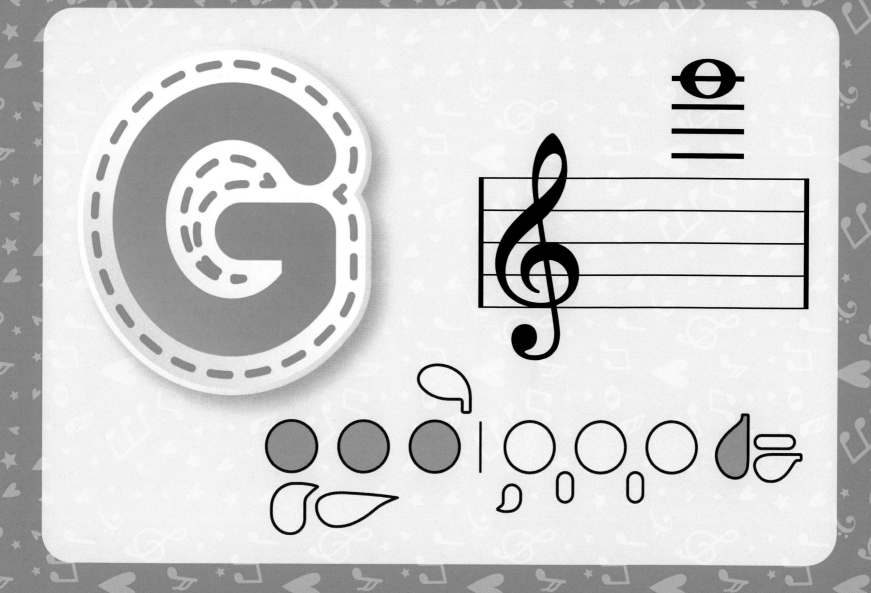

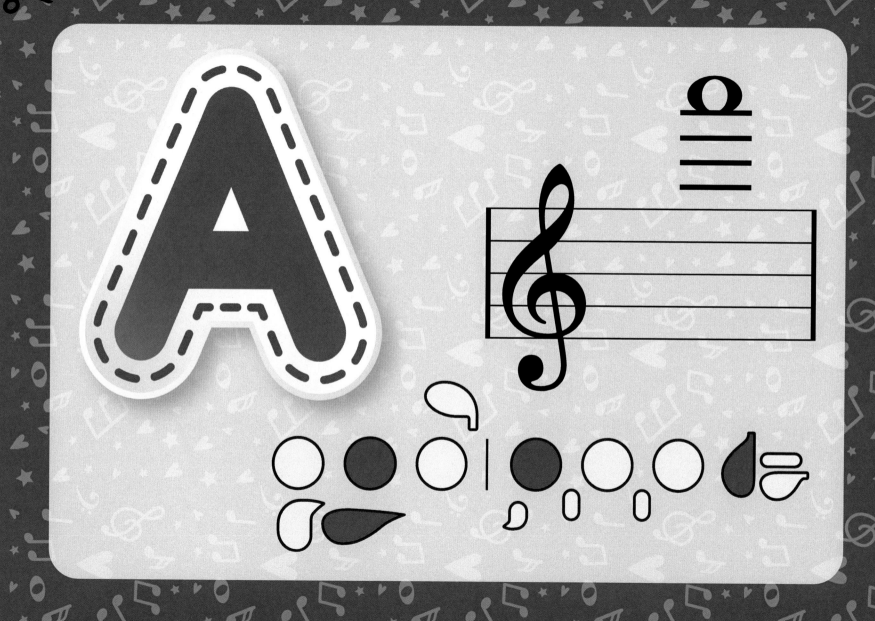

Made in the USA
Columbia, SC
17 June 2022

61857751R00046